God's Commanding Words

Gary C. Redding

God's Commanding Words

Gary C. Redding

Parson's Porch Books

Copyright (C) 2011 by Gary C. Redding

ISBN: Softcover   978-1-936912-21-6

All rights reserved. No part of this book may be reproduced or transmitted in any form or by any means, electronic or mechanical, including photocopying, recording, or by any information storage and retrieval system, without permission in writing from the publisher.

This book was printed in the United States of America.

To order additional copies of this book, contact:
Parson's Porch Books
c/o Parson's Porch, Inc
1-423-475-7308
www.parsonsporch.com

Dedicated to

my 3 girls:

my wife,

Carol,

and my daughters,

Melissa and Jennifer.

Table of Content

There is Only One God	7
Worship God Alone	21
Always Show Reverence for God	33
Get Some Rest and Let Everyone Else Have a Little, Too	45
Honor Your Family	55
Respect Life	65
Keep Marriage Sacred	75
Be Honest	85
Tell the Truth	97
Learn to be Content	107

THERE IS ONLY ONE GOD!

"I am the Lord your God, Who brought you out of Egypt, out of the land of slavery. You shall have no other gods before Me." (Exodus 20:2-3)

On February 7, 1996, in rural Hillsborough County Florida, just outside Tampa, three teenage boys drove through an intersection and directly into the path of an 8-ton truck, and were killed instantly. During the investigation, a stop sign was found lying alongside the road very near that intersection. As it turns out, earlier that same night, three other teenagers looking for something fun to do, traveled along several county roads taking down all kinds of traffic signs, including that stop sign. They were convicted of manslaughter and each faces up to 27 years in prison for the deaths of their three peers. During the sentencing, the judge told them, "I don't believe for a minute that you pulled up these signs with the intent of causing the death of anyone, but pulling up the signs caused ramifications that none of you ... ever expected."

The Ten Commandments

Whenever the Ten Commandments are mentioned, someone immediately questions their relevance to and/or their appropriateness for our time. For instance, you may remember when Ted Turner declared the Ten Commandments obsolete. Speaking to the Newspaper Association of America in Atlanta a few years ago, he said, "We're living with outmoded rules. The rules we're living under is (sic) the Ten Commandments, and I bet nobody here even pays much attention to 'em, because they are too old. When Moses went up on the mountain, there were no nuclear weapons, there was no poverty. Today, the commandments wouldn't go over. The commandments are out."

Whether Ted Turner is someone you listen to, or even respect, makes little difference. The Ten Commandments have become increasingly a matter of public debate in recent years. In 1997, Alabama Circuit Court Judge Ray Moore openly displayed the Commandments on the wall in his courtroom. His action immediately sparked both a judicial and legislative debate that continues today. In 1999, in response to widespread incidents of violence in America's public schools, even the United States House of Representatives thumbed its nose at the Supreme Court and passed a bill giving states the right to display the Ten Commandments in any public building, including schools. The debate over that bit of legislative action is ongoing, as well.

It's not my intention to join that public debate through this series of sermons. My concern is much closer to home, and more personal, than that. Frankly, I'm concerned that, without ever intending to do so, many Christian parents have, by their simple neglect to embrace and to teach their children the Ten Commandments, inflicted a devastating, and even potentially deadly blow, both to them and to civilized society. Those who ignore the Commandments, I think, are guilty of pulling up signs that point the way to godliness, decency, civility, and law and order. I don't agree that the Commandments are too old and outdated for our time. By the same token, neither do I agree that putting them on public display is all that's needed to improve the quality of life in the twenty-first century. My question is this: if the Ten Commandments are vitally important, why do we so blatantly disregard teaching and embracing them in both the private and public arenas of our lives?

To further prove my point, let me illustrate the level of ignorance of even God's people concerning the Ten Commandments. Can you answer these two questions? First, where in the Old Testament can either of the two complete listings of the Ten Commandments be found? (Answer: Exodus 20, Deuteronomy 5) Second, name the Ten Commandments, not necessarily in order. Here's a clue: the first four deal with our relationship with God; the last six deal with our relationships to each other. Have I effectively made my point?

If so, let's get started by looking at the Commandments, one by one. The first is this: "You shall have no other gods before me "(Exodus 20:3). What does that mean and why do we need to teach it to the children of the twenty-first century? Let's look at then and now and see.

First, consider the meaning and relevance of this commandment *then*. One of the first things you discover when you begin reading the Bible is that the world of the scriptures was vastly different from your world. Practically everyone you know believes in the same God. However, the biblical world was one of many gods. What's more, each god reigned over a particular area of life. For instance, when the Hebrews entered the promised land, they discovered that the folks who already lived there worshiped Baal. Baal was responsible for bringing the rains that fertilized the earth and made the crops grow. Now, what could be more important than rain when you lived in a desert region? That's why Baal was the chief god of the Canaanites and the Syrians. There were other gods, but none so important as Baal because rain was so important to their survival. For that reason, their most enthusiastic worship and most extreme obedience was reserved for Baal.

Other nations had other chief gods. The Babylonians worshiped Marduk, the storm god. The Moabites were most devoted to the sun god. Others worshiped goddesses of love and gods of war, gods of grain and of justice. Some people worshiped a national god that was believed to "belong" only to them, although their tenure was never guaranteed. National gods had to constantly prove themselves by bringing the nation victory in war and providing general prosperity and security. If they failed at that, nations were known to actually "dump" one god for another.

People didn't normally bother national gods with the trivia of daily life, primarily because they were too busy running the country to be concerned about the average Joe or Jane. So, there were "junior grade" gods who looked after the more ordinary and routine concerns of life. Besides that, many people had personal or household gods that they relied on as their "go between" or mediator with the big gods. So people had not one god but many. In addition, when they traveled to some foreign land, it was customary to worship and pay homage to the god of that land so that he would not unleash some unfortunate accident against them while they were in his territory.

All of this sounds pretty foolish and superstitious to us, but it was deadly serious business in the Old Testament. That's why the Hebrews would have found the first commandment so hard to swallow. The Lord was asking them to give up all those other gods and worship Him alone. That means they were supposed to pray to Him and to rely upon Him for everything! It meant that the common person could pray to the Lord, just as a priest and king could. It even meant that if they all prayed at the same time, this God of the first commandment could hear every one of them share with Him even the most minute details of daily life. He knew about everything from childbirth and farming to love and justice and war. They didn't need any other gods if they simply pledged their allegiance to Him. That's what the first commandment was all about.

Obeying the first commandment might sound like a piece of cake to you and me, but the commandment was really hard to swallow way back when. In return for their exclusive worship and loyalty, God promised to supply everything they ever needed. He had already demonstrated His love for them: He brought them out of Egypt and gave them a land to call their very own. Now, they would be His special possession, as long as He was their only God.

Second, consider the meaning and relevance of this commandment *now*. Granted, our world is different from either the Old or New Testament worlds! Most people don't worship multiple gods or think of gods as specialists to be consulted only on matters related to their unique abilities or assigned responsibilities. However, our world does present a different set of dilemmas related to the first commandment. For instance, we live in closer contact with people of different religions than ever before. We may have neighbors who are Jewish, Hindu, Buddhist, Muslim, or nothing at all. Because of that, schools may ignore religious holidays altogether, or observe the holidays of different religions in alternating years, all in the name of cultural diversity. In fact, the likelihood of that happening is increasing. According to some recent polls, there are now more Muslims and Buddhists in America than Episcopalians. That's why Christians must be diligent to teach our children and grandchildren the relevance of this commandment to the world in which they live.

So, let me explain the twenty-first century relevance of this commandment by addressing three questions that I am routinely asked. They're questions that take on greater urgency simply because Muslims and Jews do move into our neighborhoods and Hindus do practice their religion in front of us. *So, here's the first question: Although we may call Him something different, do we not all worship and serve the same God?* Those who ask the question often follow it up like this: we call Him God, Muslims call him Allah, and I've even heard one or two acquaintances refer to him as Shang-ti. Isn't it just like what we do with water? Americans ask for water, Spanish ask for agua. It's like that with God, isn't it? The words and names are different, but we all have the same supreme being in mind.

I simply can't agree with that argument. The clearest way to underscore the difference between the Christian faith and other religions is in what each one claims about Jesus. The Bible asserts that Jesus is God's "one and only begotten Son"(John 3:16). It says that "He is the image of the invisible of God" (Colossians 1: 15). Jesus Himself said that "1 and the Father are one"(John 10:30), and that "Anyone who has seen Me has seen the Father"(John 14:9). Jesus stated emphatically that, "I am the way, the truth, and the life. No one can come to the Father except through Me"(John 14:6). The Apostle Peter said that "Salvation is found in no one else, for there is no other name under heaven given to men by which we must be saved" (Acts 4: 12).

"Don't we all worship the same God?" If that is the question, then the answer has to be, "Tell me what other religions say about Jesus and I'll tell you then whether we worship the same God." Here it is from scripture: "This is how you can recognize the Spirit of God: every Spirit that acknowledges that Jesus Christ has come in the flesh is from God, but every spirit that does not acknowledge Jesus in not from God" (I John 4:2-3). Answers don't often come that directly or that clearly, but with regard to Jesus, they do! If we choose to believe that the Christian faith is just one way among many to look at God, no better or no worse than any other, we aren't holding to the faith of the scriptures. We are, in fact, creating a religion of our own.

If a religious faith, whether its origins are in some foreign country, or its practitioners grew up with you and have been known to you since childhood, if a religious faith claims anything else or anything less about Jesus than that He is the one and only begotten Son of God, only Savior of the world, the sovereign Lord of lords, and the everlasting King of all kings, then that faith is not the Christian faith, is not equal to the Christian faith, and that person does not worship the God of the Ten Commandments or the God revealed in the Christian scriptures. The God we worship claims Jesus as His One and Only Son. A faith that claims less for Jesus does not represent the God we worship. It is that plain and simple!

The second question I am routinely asked: does it really matter what religion a person practices, or what god a person worships? Listen to me. Some things don't matter one bit. I may say "toe-may-toe" and you may say "toe-mah-toe" and we simply agree to disagree. We may disagree on the significance of some historical event, political candidate, or the meaning of some work of art. Some things just don't have a definite right and wrong answer. However, if we're driving down the road and I say the traffic light is red and you say it's green, we could be heading for disaster! There are some things that do matter and therefore, they have to be settled.

If the truth about God falls into the category of debatable issues, if the religion one practices, the God one worships, or the things that a person believes don't matter, we'd all be better off just leaving each other alone. The fact, though, is that the truth about God matters more than anything else. Current world events demonstrate that. We become like the god we worship, and we also allow this god to determine the kind of world we give shape to, the kind of government we will establish, and what sorts of persons we want to lead us, or to rule over us. The god we choose determines what kind of work we will do, how we will feel about it, what we will think of, and how we will treat our bodies. And, of course, the god we choose determines what we think of other people, of friendships and other human relationships. If our god is cheap, shoddy, and easily manipulated, we'll treat people the same way. We become the choices we make. We become just like the god we choose to worship and the religion we determine to practice. Yes, religious faith and God matter!

The final question I'm frequently asked that relates to this first commandment is this: isn't it mean and even un-Christ like to be so intolerant of other faiths? Shouldn't we learn how to accept each other's beliefs and find some way to get along since we do live in such a global community? I'm glad you ask that question.

I worry sometimes that in our world the worst sin has become the sin of intolerance. There was a time in the not-too-distant past when intolerance meant bigotry and prejudice. People who disagreed with the majority viewpoint or, who were a part of a minority racial, ethnic, religious, or political group, were often treated with meanness, hostility, and even violence. That day is hopefully past. In fact, such responses to differing viewpoints should offend us all and should be rejected outright, especially by the people of God. Remember, our Lord said that the power of our love is the greatest witness of our faith and our relationship to Him (John 13:35).

However, in our efforts to reject mean-spirited intolerance, I'm afraid that we've embraced tolerance to a fault. In our world, tolerance has become the chief virtue; tolerance is more important than truth. Whoever or whatever a person wants to worship or believe is what's most important. The sacredness of individual choice is the highest good. Truth is whatever makes a person feel good, and of course, different things make different people feel good. So, truth is always changing because it's always individualized. That means what whatever a person believes is true must be respected by the rest of us. Listen to me. That whole idea is nothing but a fresh variety of paganism.

There is only one God. He is the God of the Ten Commandments, the God of the scriptures, the God revealed most fully in Jesus Christ Love those who believe differently than you do. That's the new commandment, the additional commandment that our Lord gives to us. Treat those who differ from you with kindness, gentleness, and mercy. Don't be condescending toward them. Don't treat them with contempt or hostility. Don't even argue with them, but be obedient to the scriptures when they say: *"Always be prepared to give an answer to everyone who asks you to give the reason for the hope that you have. But do this with gentleness and respect "(1 Peter 3: 15).*

Listen to the Word of God. *" I have set before you lift and death, blessings and curses. Now choose lift, so that you and your children may live and that you may love the Lord your God, listen to His voice, and hold fast to Him. For the Lord is your lift ... "*(Deuteronomy 30: 19-20). God knows what you're looking and longing for in life. God knows what you desperately and truly need. He is the Only One Who can meet that need and He has set before you in His commands the key to life. He is the only God you need. Never put another god before Him!

WORSHIP GOD ALONE!

"You shall not make for yourself an idol in the form of anything in heaven above or on the Earth beneath or in the waters below. You shall not bow down to them or worship them; for I, the Lord your God, am a jealous God, punishing the children for the sin of the fathers to the third and fourth generation of those who hate Me, but showing love to a thousand generations of those who love Me and keep My commandments." (Exodus 20:4)

Some people claim that the second commandment is the most outdated and useless, the most primitive and irrelevant, of the Ten Commandments. What do you think? It prohibits making graven images, or idols, and then bowing down to worship. Quite frankly, I doubt that very few of you have ever laid your eyes on an idol, much less actually seen someone in the act of worshiping one. However, before you cast your vote on whether this commandment is needed or relevant, maybe you should hear this.

The First *Presleyterian* Church of Elvis the Divine was organized in Denver in 1988, eleven years after the death of Elvis Presley, the king of rock n' roll. Since then, pockets of Elvis worship have taken hold in New York, New

The Ten Commandments

Jersey, Indiana, and a handful of other states. In fact, more than twenty-five years after he died, Elvis worship continues to spread across the globe. The tenets of *Presleyterianism* are simple: eat six meals a day with frequent snacking in between; face Las Vegas once a day; make at least one pilgrimage during your lifetime to Qraceland; and, finally, fight always against the evil anti-Elvis, Michael Jackson.

The founder of the church, Rev. Mark Farndu, admits that it all started out as a joke, a simple marketing ploy designed to make lots of money. Soon, though, it got out of hand: serious-minded followers of Elvis began gathering and holding so-called "services." They believe that Elvis watches over them. When someone reports seeing Presley, the high priests of yet another Elvis-centered gathering in Denver, the Church of the Risen Elvis, hold Presley worship services. They have even enshrined a look-alike Elvis doll in an altar surrounded by candles and flowers. What's more, they post the King's 31 Commandments on the walls of their meeting rooms.

Apparently, idolatry is alive and well in America, even in the twentieth and twenty-first centuries! While it takes all kinds of people, including lots of very strange ones, to make the world go 'round, unfortunately it's not just the fringe element who need to pay attention to the second commandment. Because of the kind of world we live in, our children need to be taught it and we definitely need to remember to observe it. Let me tell you why I believe this second commandment hits us all right where we live.

First, we keep this commandment because of what it reveals about idols(v.4,· Exodus 32:1-5). You remember that Moses climbed Mt. Sinai to receive the Ten Commandments from God. According to the scriptures, altogether Moses was on the mountain for more than a month, forty days and nights to be precise(Exodus 24:18). As he lingered there, the people began to suspect the worst, what with all the smoke and fire hovering around the top of the mountain, along with the occasional rumble of an earthquake(Exodus 32:1). "Who knows?" some of them must have thought, "Maybe the Lord got made and decided to get rid of Moses. And without Moses, where does that leave us? We don't really know the Lord that well yet; certainly not as well as Moses knows Him. We know that God has done some great things for us, but life's pretty uncertain right now. What if He's left us, too? It's one thing to think that Moses might not come back, but if God has left us we'll be stuck out here in the middle of nowhere with no God to save us. What will we do then?"

That's the way people think, isn't it? Let a baby lose sight of everyone in the house, and he screams for reassurance that he's not alone. Let a friend be out of touch for a while; you'll wonder if you've been dropped. Let a spouse, a parent, or child, withdraw from meaningful contact into an isolated shell of their own making; you'll start to worry, too. We all need something concrete and tangible, something real, some evidence that we can see with our own eyes, touch with our own hands, hear with our own ears, some proof that we are loved and we have not been abandoned. If we can't get it, then we begin to think just like the Hebrews.

It had been more than a month since they heard from Moses and Moses was the most tangible evidence of God that they had. Every other nation surrounding them, even the wandering tribes of nomads they encountered during their wilderness journey, had their gods. Did the absence of Moses mean that they were without their God?

That's probably when some quick thinker came up with a bright idea. "We can make our own god. Who needs Moses anyhow? Aaron, Moses' brother, can be our leader. Aaron, make a god for us so we can get out of this fix your brother got us into."

The scriptures make it clear that the people wanted another god(32:1). Remember last week: I told you that it wasn't unusual for nations and tribes to switch gods if the one they worshiped didn't come through for them. Well, the people were ready to switch! What's more, Aaron appears to oblige them. He takes up a collection of all their gold, melts it down, and fashions a calf from it. As soon as they see it, they begin to worship it, saying, "These are your gods, O Israel, who brought you up out of Egypt "(32:4).

The text suggests, though, Aaron never intended to create a new god for the people. His point to Moses was that his intentions were honorable. He realized the people were more than ready to go after some false god, but he only wanted to give them some tangible representation of the Lord God so they wouldn't turn away from Him. In fact, when he saw them worshiping the idol, Aaron specifically told the people, "Tomorrow there will be a festival to the Lord"(v.5).

It wasn't unlike what Rev. Mark Farndu ran into when he organized the First *Presleyterian* Church of Denver. He never intended to start such a ridiculous new religious movement. It was only a joke to him, just a way to make money. Little did he know that people would take him seriously. But before he knew it, it got way out of hand and he found himself in the same boat with Aaron.

Let me tell you something about this second commandment: we violate it most often without ever intending to violate it at all. Merely trying to prevent one wrong, we find ourselves committing another. What starts out in our mind and heart as one thing, what began innocently as a sincere effort to do the right and honorable thing, suddenly becomes a monster, something else entirely from what we had in mind.

Let me show you what I mean. You've heard the old story about a little child who was hard at work with her crayons and paper. Her mother observed her intense concentration and asked, "What are you drawing, honey?" "I'm drawing God," the child replied matter-of-factly. "But sweetheart," the mother said, "nobody has ever seen God. Nobody knows what He looks like." The child never looked up from her work as she confidently replied, "Yes, I know. But they will when I'm done!"

So it is with many of us. We take our images of God, our thoughts about Him, our experiences of and with Him, so seriously that we run the risk of mistaking those images for the real thing. In fact, sometimes, those images become so important to us, they actually become like god to us.

We become threatened, argumentative, defensive, and even combative if others don't see God the way we do, if they don't understand Him, if they haven't experienced Him exactly like we do, the way we have. Our way becomes for us, the only way anyone can legitimately look at and think of, worship or serve, our God. That's as much the sin of idolatry as anything else. In fact, I think it may be the most common form of idolatry among the people of God in our time.

Have you ever thought that sometimes our concept of God is much too incomplete, entirely too limited and confined, and too incredibly small? If our image of God is small, it will be hard to imagine God being able to solve all our problems, hear all our prayers, and ultimately to do in our lives and in our world what seems impossible, which is what often must be done in order to solve all our problems. Likewise, if our image of God is of an old, white man, we may find it difficult to believe that God is just as much the God of red, yellow, black, and brown people, or that He even has a heart for the females and the young among us.

My point is this: an idol is any image we create of God, even in our minds, which threatens to become a substitute for our God. The second commandment orders us not to do that! If you want to know what God is really like, look full in the wonderful face of Jesus. The scriptures tell us that "He is the exact image of the invisible God"(Colossians 1:15). When it comes to God, Jesus leaves nothing in doubt!

Second, we keep this commandment because of what it reveals about God(v.5). God follows up the commandment by revealing why He is so opposed, not just to making idols of false gods but also to trying to concoct or create images of the living God. "I, the Lord your God, am a jealous God. .. , " He says(v.5). That's a pretty shocking statement, isn't it? Of all the attributes that you could ascribe to God were someone to ask, most would never think of characterizing the Lord God asjealous. Among us, it's just not a character trait that's much admired. In fact, it conjures up such negative emotions, what could God possibly mean and ever hope to gain by describing Himself in such a way? It really is a good question; one, though, that is not difficult to explain.

Let me ask all you married people something: whose picture do you carry in your wallet? It really should only be your wife or your husband, and your children. How would they feel if you kept some other woman's picture, and the pictures of her children, in your wallet? Hurt, to say the least. Probably angry, and jealous as well. Marriage is an exclusive relationship between one man and one woman for a lifetime. Flirtations with others than your spouse, deep friendships where intimacies are shared that should be shared only within the context of marriage, and affairs of the heart and body, constitute adultery. In fact, if you love anyone or anything more than your husband or wife, if you allow anyone or anything to distract your full attention from your husband or wife, is, from the biblical perspective, adultery. In the Bible, idolatry is also called adultery towards God.

The reason God is jealous is simply because He has made an exclusive commitment to us, His people. He will not play second fiddle to an idol or to anything else in your life and mine. Period. That's why He gave the first commandment: "You will have no other gods before me." It's why He gave the second commandment: "You will not bow down before any idols." In other words, if you belong to me, then you must not worship what other people worship! Furthermore, you must be content with the image of Me revealed in my Son Jesus Christ, and you must never try to add to or take away from Who and What He shows Me to be like.

We break this commandment a lot, you and I. Do you remember what I said earlier about Aaron's sin being our sin? We're good people, and we want to do the right and honorable things. What could be more honorable than to work hard, and long if necessary? Even if our work, or our weariness from work, takes us out of worship, Bible study, and fellowship with other believers. Working hard is honorable, and so is taking care of ourselves. And so, work comes between us and God.

Likewise, what could be more honorable than providing for our family, paying all our bills on time, and establishing good credit, plenty of credit? Surely, God wants us to fulfill all our financial obligations. Often, though, we dishonor God by taking on more than we can handle, and then we further complicate our dishonor, but having nothing left to give to Him. So, our financial obligations and good credit come between us and God.

Listen to me. It doesn't have to be that way. If we get the first two commandments in order, then our lives will likely come together in ways we have never experienced before! I heard about a preacher who spoke at a downtown, inner city church. He was the special guest for the day. The service began at 11:00 am. and included several testimonies, announcements, six hymns, along with a number of soloists and choral presentations. It did not conclude until 1:15 p.m.

After the service the guest preacher asked the pastor why his service was so long. He smiled and said, "Unemployment down here runs nearly 50 percent. For our youth, unemployment is much higher. That means that during a typical week, everything down here tells our people, 'You're a failure. You're nobody. You're no good. And it's all because you don't have a good job or a fine car; it's all because you have no money."

"So we gather here once a week, and get our heads straight. In the hymns, the prayers, the testimonies, and the sermon, we tell them, 'What you're hearing out there in the world is lie, a big awful lie! You are somebody! You are God's people. He has bought you with a price and He loves you.' It takes us so long to worship because the world has perverted them so much, and we have to get their heads straight."

That's what worshiping God does. It gets our heads on straight. It reminds us of the truth and helps identify the lies and the false gods of this world. When you bow down before God, when you truly worship Him, your head and your thinking, your heart and your living will get straight.

There's just one more thing about this commandment: we keep it because of what it reveals about you and me(v.5-6). Several hundred years after this commandment was given, the prophet Jeremiah appeared on the scene. He could look back over the history of God's people and see the awful consequences of idolatry. Listen to this warning; it's one of the most frightening things in scripture. Jeremiah said, "They followed worthless idols and they became worthless themselves"(2:5). We become exactly like the gods we worship.

Several hundred years after Jeremiah, the Apostle Paul looked at the span of history between himself and the prophet. He said: "They ... changed the glory of the incorruptible God into an image made like corruptible man, and to birds and four-footed beasts, and creeping things; ... they exchanged, or substituted the truth of God for a lie, and worshiped and served the creature more than the Creator" (Romans 1:23,25). We're still doing it, you know. What's more, the very nature of the gods we worship is still being reflected in the ways we live. Let me see any man or woman as they really are, give me just a glance, just the briefest insight into their true personality, and I'll know a wealth of information about the god they worship.

The commandment says that the consequences of breaking this commandment will last from one generation to another. You better hear that, my friends. It is the Word of the Lord God Himself. What you decide to do with Him will come back to reward or haunt you for years to come! Ame

ALWAYS SHOW REVERENCE FOR GOD

"You shall not misuse the name of the Lord your God, for the Lord will not hold anyone Guiltless who misuses His name." (Exodus 20:5)

One of the first struggles that new parents face is the incredibly difficult decision about what to name their child. When you realize that it will stay with your son or daughter for the rest of their life, it takes on monumental significance. You want to choose a name that you like; more importantly, you want to choose a name they like, one they will be happy to keep.

Some of you may remember the old Johnny Cash song, "A Boy Named Sue." A man named his little boy Sue, then shortly thereafter abandoned the family. The boy made it his life's goal to find his father and make him pay for "sticking" him with such an awful name. When he eventually finds his father, he says to him, "My name is Sue, how do you do? Now, you're gonna' die." Have you always liked your name? Or, have you sometimes felt like the boy named Sue?

Fortunately, most parents get it right. Some others, though, well, you just have to wonder what they were thinking. For instance, former Texas Governor James Hogg actually named his daughter "Ima." For many years, a story circulated that there was another sister named Ura Hogg. Thankfully, that proved to be untrue: there was only one daughter, Ima Hogg. A couple not far from here whose last name was "Fail," named their twin sons "Will" and "Won't;" names which, by the way, turned out to be prophetic.

I read about a window washer in Montreal who accidentally fell as he was washing the windows of a downtown skyscraper. His name was Will Drop. There was a baseball coach named Joe Bunt, and a barber named Dan Druff. O'Neill and Pray were partners in a company that manufactured church furnishings. A plaster contractor was named Will Crumble. Then there's retired boxer George Foreman who has 11 sons, all of whom are named "George." Go figure. You may remember a couple of years ago that the rapper Puff Daddy changed his name to P. Diddy. Within minutes, Andy Rooney of 60 Minutes announced that he was changing his name to Puff Daddy; thankfully, it was a threat he never carried out. Obviously, though, some people should consider changing their name.

In the third commandment, God takes steps to protect His name. He demands that His people always show His name proper respect and reverence. The King James Version reads: "Thou shalt not take the name of the Lord thy God in vain; for the Lord will not hold him guiltless that taketh His name in vain"(Exodus 20:7). The NIV reads: "You shall not misuse the name of the Lord your God, for the Lord will not hold anyone guiltless who misuses His name. " What does this commandment mean and what are its expectations of us? In a world that seems to have lost its capacity for reverence and respect, what does the third commandment really mean? That is what this sermon is about: a vital truth we need to recover, and one which every child needs to learn. Let's get started.

First, the commandment clearly states that it is permissible to use God's name, but it is never permissible to abuse it In fact, the Bible goes to great lengths to warn people about mishandling God's name. Leviticus 24:16 pronounces the death penalty upon anyone guilty of doing so. In biblical days, the people of God took extreme measures to insure that they did not violate this commandment.

The Ten Commandments

You know that the Hebrew scriptures were written originally with no vowels, only consonants, don't you? Over time, the more educated Hebrews became afraid that people might give up reading the scriptures altogether because in the absence of vowels, it was often difficult to decipher what word a series of consonants might represent. So, they added vowels, but they would not place them between the consonants. Instead, they used combinations of dots and comma-like markings called "jots and tittles" and inserted them at the appropriate places above and below and a little off to the side of the consonants. However, when they came to the four consonants for the name of God, YHWH, they inserted no vowels. They felt that would be sacrilegious. They were fearful that, without even intending to do so, they might add to or take something away from His name and thereby, break the third commandment. They were so careful, in fact, of how they handled the name of God, Jews refused to even try to pronounce the name, YHWH: translated into English as Yahweh or Jehovah.

What's more, in ancient biblical times, it was not even permitted to write the name of God in ink unless you were one of the scribes whose professional duty it was to copy the scriptures. Even then, when a scribe came to the word for God, YHWH, he would take a complete bath before writing it. Then he would put on clothes that had

The Ten Commandments

never been worn. After that, he would get a quill which had never had a drop of ink on it. Only then would he write God's name and, after he finished, he would destroy the quill so that it could never write anything else. What's more, he would throwaway the clothes he had worn when writing God's name so that they could never be worn again. That is how deeply the name of God was revered and respected in the ancient Hebrew world.

How different it is in our culture! For instance, a couple of mothers were talking not long ago about teaching their children the appropriate time to use, along with the appropriate manner to say, inappropriate words. (Yes, they were talking about teaching their children how to "cuss," because "it's the only way to get along in today's world.") I hope they do not represent the norm. In fact, I am still naive enough to believe that every family should have a list of unacceptable words, words that members of that family are not ever permitted to use. They are bad words. Some of them even crop up in conversation when you read the Bible. "Daddy, is hell a bad word?" What do you say when you are asked that? How about, "That's a good question, and it depends on how you use it." Let me try to help you a little more. What you should impress upon your children, and what this commandment speaks to is this: always be careful what you say. Don't ever use bad words, but more importantly, do not use perfectly good words badly. The Bible tells us not to misuse God's name. On the other hand, the scriptures tell us that we are to use God's name in worship, in adoration, and in praise. For instance, we read in Psalm 8:1: "O Lord, our Lord, how majestic is Your Name in all the earth." In Psalm 103:1, we read: "Bless the Lord, O my soul, and all that is within me, bless His holy Name." And, in Acts 4: 12, we are told: "Salvation is found in no one else, for there is no other name under heaven given to men by which we must be saved"(Acts 4: 12).

It's true, we can either honor or dishonor God; either show our respect and our reverence for Him, or our complete disregard and contempt for Him, by the ways in which we use His name. This commandment tells us to take great care in the way we use God's name. In fact, don't be so careless in using it. Be aware of every time the name of God crosses your lips. The Bible says there are long-term consequences which follow our decision to either respect or disregard His name.

Second, this commandment teaches us to hallow God's name, not hollow it o/its meaning. Not long ago, someone tried to steal my identity. Maybe it's happened to you; certainly you have heard of it happening to others. Identity thieves don't require a lot of information, but if they can get the "right" information from or about you, they can make your life miserable for a very long time. In fact, if they're good enough and quick enough, by the next morning, you may not even be you; overnight, someone else might become you, and everything you have ever worked for could become theirs. As for me, I spent the better part of one recent Friday afternoon and evening trying to recover compromised personal data and attempting to re-establish some kind of personal security in my life. I did everything I was supposed to do, but I may not ever know for sure if I was successful.

The third commandment sounds a warning: "Do not hollow God's name of its meaning." In other words, do not rob God's name of its power and significance. Do not use His name in any way that would cause others to question His existence, His nature, or His character. In our contemporary cultural setting, this commandment literally means, "do not steal God's identity and make use of it for your own personal gain or advantage." Rather, we are to remember that Jesus taught us in the Lord's prayer to hallow His name by upholding it in reverence(Matthew 6:9); and to do so, not merely while we are praying or worshiping, but while we are actually living out our days in an irreverent world and working hard to meaningfully put together this thing called life.

You have seen how people rob names of their meaning. How many times have you noted about some friend or family member, "Well, he calls himself a

Republican, or a conservative, but he sure doesn't sound like one?" Or, "He claims to be patriotic, but why is he so critical of our President? If he really is as patriotic as he says, why wasn't he more supportive of the war in Iraq?" You see, even we realize that actions must be consistent with the names and labels we wear. Have you ever seen a married man or woman in some compromising situation and wondered whether their wedding vows, or the ring on their finger, means anything at all to them? Have you never wondered about someone, "Well, I know she's a member of the church, but I never thought that a Christian talked like that or carried on like she does?" In every situation which comes up, you're acknowledging that the individual in question has completely robbed of its meaning the very thing they claim to be, the very thing they most want to be.

It's tragic, but it sometimes has an amusing side to it. Watch guys in particular, who insist on wearing athletic garb which prominently displays the names and numbers of their most admired sports hero. You've seen it a hundred times: the most awkward guy on the basketball team insists on wearing Michael Jordan's number. It happens a lot in "old men's" softball and touch football leagues: men trying to hold on to their youth, wanting desperately to believe they may yet become something they never were. Be honest, guys: how many golfers who wear a shirt and a cap with the Nike logo or play with Nike golf balls, have ever been transformed into Tiger Woods?

We show utter disregard and complete disrespect for God when we use His name but refuse to allow Him to transform our lives. We hollow His name of all its power and significance when we plaster His name on our business signs or business cards, but then fail to build and conduct our business according to the principles of God's word. We steal His identity and use it for our own gain when we fail to treat our customers and clients with the respect and kindness that is consistent with His character.

We as believers, are marked with God's seal. That means that our every word, our every action, our every thought bears God's mark on it. That being so, the question then becomes, "Do our words, our actions, and our thoughts make good use of God's name? Do they represent Him well? Is He proud that we bear His name?" Whether we like it or not, everything we do as believers, represents Him. If it does not represent Him well or rightly, then we are guilty of violating this third commandment.

Finally, this commandment teaches us to hold the name of God in highest acclaim and never to profane it. Did you see that Bill Cosby was in town last Sunday speaking to the class of 2003 at Paine College? Did you happen to read the report of his remarks in the Monday edition of *The Augusta Chronicle*? For starters, Cosby told the graduates and thousands of spectators that he worries about the "vulgar" music young people listen to these days. "When I'm riding in my car," he said, "and some ... youngsters are driving along, I can feel their car coming . ... And the language coming of that car is something I didn't ask for."

Now, hear me. Bill Cosby's remarks registered a valid and much needed complaint both about the loud volume of music coming out of today's automobiles, as well as the vulgar lyrics. And believe me, none of us ask for it. The fact is, we live in a culture marked by rudeness, crudeness, disgust, vulgarity, profanity, and incivility. We live in a society that seems to feed, and even thrive, on "trash talk." What's most unbelievable about it is how many Christians engage in that kind of talk.

Listen to what the scriptures say about how we talk. "Do not let any unwholesome talk come out of your mouth, " wrote the Apostle Paul. James, the brother of our Lord, wrote: "With the tongue we praise our Lord and Father, and with it we curse men, who have been made in God's likeness. Out of the same mouth come praise and cursing. My brothers, this should not be"(3:9-lO). That is exactly what this third commandments forbids among the people of God.

The Ten Commandments

Maybe you don't understand what's wrong with profanity. The word "profane" means "debasing, degrading, or defiling that which is holy or worthy of reverence." So, to profane something that is perfect and holy and sacred means to take it and yank it down to our level, or even lower. Did you hear about the hazing incident in the Chicago-area high school last weekend? Senior girls attacked junior girls following a powder puff football game, kicked them, punched them, threw bottles, tubs, cans, and paint at them, pushed them down and then smeared fish guts and human feces into their faces. That was degrading, humiliating, and profaning the girls who suffered that torment. It is the same thing that we do to God when we profane His name. We take the Holy Name of our God and we bring it down to the level of trash and filth in our world. In the words of the brother of our Lord, "This should not be. "

Let me tell you something. You wouldn't dare stand by and allow anyone to say something bad about your mother. You wouldn't stand for them dragging her name in the mud, and you would never think of doing so yourself. Why, then, would you engage in such "trash talk" about your Heavenly Father? I'm not just talking about using God's name in connection with some other word of profanity. I'm talking about such common, ordinary, everyday expressions like, "Oh, my God!" and "Jesus! What'd you do that for?"

We are God's people and we should bend over backwards to treat the name of our God with respect.and reverence. I tell you what. I give you all permission right now. The next time you smash your finger with a hammer, or hit an errant shot on the golf course, or break your favorite plate, or get angry with the driver of another car, your mate, or one of your children, I give you permission to say, "Oh, Gary Redding!" Or even, "Oh, George Bush!" Go to whatever extreme you have to, just don't profane the name of our God. There is no other name in all the universe like that name!

GET SOME REST AND LET EVERYONE ELSE HAVE A LITTLE, TOO!

"Remember the Sabbath day by keeping it holy. Six days you shall labor and do all your work, but the seventh day is a Sabbath to the Lord your God. On it you shall not do any work, neither you, nor your son or daughter, nor your manservant or maidservant, nor your animals, nor the alien within your gate. For in six days the Lord made the heavens and the earth, the sea, and all that is in them, but He rested on the seventh day. Therefore the Lord blessed the Sabbath day and made it holy." (Exodus 20:8-11)

A friend who owns an automotive repair shop in Augusta recently told me about a customer who drives a pick-up truck with over 400,000 miles on its engine. What's more, not one single major repair has been necessary during the lifetime of that truck. When I marveled at the thought of it and asked how anyone could possibly put that many miles on any non-commercial vehicle, he replied with a single word: maintenance.

That shouldn't come as a surprise to any of us. The importance of proper maintenance to the life of any mechanical thing is a well-known fact. For our cars to last, we must periodically and regularly change the oil and oil filter, rotate the tires, lubricate practically everything on it that moves, tune the engine, and routinely replace worn parts. If we do proper maintenance, the car will last a lot longer than if we don't.

That's what the fourth commandment is about: not maintaining your car, mind you, but properly maintaining yourself. It's called the law of the Sabbath and once you understand it, you'll marvel at how relevant and practical to the pace of life today is this mandate given by the Lord more than 3,000 years ago. This law contains a truth that practically guarantees a longer, healthier, more productive and more fulfilling life. Interested? Then, let's get started.

The place for a Christian to begin is with Jesus' understanding of the law of the Sabbath (Mark 2:23-28). In His day the rules about how to keep the Sabbath had become so complicated and burdensome that they actually worked against God's original purpose in establishing a day for rest. For instance, it was generally understood that there were 39 different categories of work at which persons could legitimately labor. Religious leaders in Jesus' day analyzed those 39 different categories of occupation and developed a list of 1,521 specific tasks related to them which couldn't be done on the Sabbath.

For instance, you couldn't look in a mirror on the Sabbath. Why? Because you might see a gray hair and be tempted to yank it out of your head or eyebrow and that was considered work too closely related to shearing sheep. You could dip a radish in salt on the Sabbath but if you did, you had to eat it quickly because it would begin to pickle and that would be work. On the Sabbath, it was forbidden to tie a knot, except with one hand It was forbidden to light a fire, to move a lamp, to go on a journey longer than 3/4 of a mile, a distance referred to in Acts 1:12 as "a Sabbath day's walk." Some interpretations of the law of the Sabbath were so extreme that they simply defied all reason. For instance, the Maccabean Jews were so conservative that they would stand and be killed in cold blood by Roman soldiers rather than take up arms and defend themselves on the Sabbath. For them, keeping this law was dearer than life itself.

Even healing was forbidden on the Sabbath. If someone became ill or got injured, steps could be taken to keep them from getting worse, but it wasn't permitted to give them treatment on the Sabbath that could make them better or cure them. That would have to wait for a day.

Ordinary people couldn't hope to ever get it right Even Jesus never got it right in the eyes of some. They were constantly on His back about the things He did on the Sabbath that they didn't consider permissible; things like healing, or He and His disciples casually feeding themselves on dry grain as they cut through a field on a Sabbath day's walk.

That's when Jesus explained His Father's purpose in establishing the Sabbath. "This day was made for you, " He said, "you weren't made for it" (Mark 2:27). In other words, God set aside the day for your benefit, but you've made it a burden. God meant for you to relax on the Sabbath, but you've made the day such a source of anxiety that people can't relax for fear of doing something wrong. Then He said, "Listen to me. I am the Lord of the Sabbath"(Mark 2:28), meaning, of course, that His was the definitive word on what God intends people to do with the Sabbath.

I grew up in a culture not :far removed in attitude from the one in which Jesus lived. The first pastor I remember is Rev. Idus Barnette, who was well-known for his strict and uncompromising view of the Sabbath. According to him, Christians should never patronize businesses that were open on Sunday, and that especially included restaurants. To eat out on Sunday required that other people work to prepare and serve your food. However, all food preparation for Sunday meals at home, along with ironing, polishing shoes, and other preparation for Sunday should be done the night before. Boys and girls should keep on their church clothes all day to make certain they behaved appropriately on "the Lord's day." It was all right to play six days a week, but never on Sunday. I always figured that Brother Idus' Bible didn't have all the teachings of Jesus in it, especially the ones about the Sabbath. It's hard to miss or misinterpret how Jesus viewed the Sabbath.

Second, in light of Jesus' teaching regarding the Sabbath, it's helpful for Christians to re-examine the fourth commandment. In doing so, there are three things you should notice. First, contrary to what most people believe, "Sabbath" does not mean seventh. It does, in fact, though, mean "to cease, desist, or rest." It comes from the verb used in the creation account to describe what God did on the seventh day of creation(Genesis 2:2): He rested!

For the people of God, every living thing in Israel would cease, desist, and rest from their normal work for one entire day out of every seven. That included children, slaves, livestock, even foreigners and immigrants who lived among the people of God. Eventually, the law of the Sabbath was expanded to even include the land: one year out of every seven, the land should be given a rest from planting(Leviticus 25:1-7).

I recalled the sabbatical year on this past Thursday on the 50th anniversary of the conquest of Mt. Everest, the highest peak on earth. Eighty-three-year-old Sir Edmund Hillary, the first man known to have stood on the top of the world, was in Nepal for the celebration. Since he did it in 1953, more than 1,200 people from 63 countries have reached the summit. The youngest was 15, the oldest was 70. The fastest scaled the 29,035 foot peak in 10 hours, 56 minutes. One climber has been to the top 13 times. More than 500 were on the mountain trying to reach the top of the world in time for Thursday's celebration. It's almost routine now, it seems. Practically anyone with approximately $65,000 to spend can get there. That's why on Thursday, Sir Edmund Hillary said, "It's time to give the mountain a rest." I thought, "That's the principle of the Sabbath." According to the scriptures, everyone and everything, including the earth and its mountain peaks, needs a break.

Second, the commandment requires that we keep the Sabbath holy. We've talked before about this notion of holiness. The word simply means "different or distinct from," or "special and unique when compared to" every thing else that seems to be like it. For instance, even though your fine china, crystal, and silverware fall into the category of eating utensils, to you, they are special and unique. You don't use them everyday and you don't host your family to ordinary meals served on them. They're reserved for special and extraordinary occasions. In a sense, that makes them holy!

So it is with the Sabbath. "Six days you shall labor and do all your work, " God says, but one day in seven is to be set aside as completely different from the rest. You are not to work on that day. You're to rest and to allow everything else in your life to be at rest, too.

The Sabbath is to be a radical change of pace for you. It's "Stop-and-take-a-breath-day." It's whole purpose is "time out." It's intended purely to prevent burnout! It's the principle of maintenance, that same principle to which my mechanic friend referred. "If you take care of it better, it'll last longer."

You respond, "That would be nice, but there's just not enough time in a day, even in six days, to do everything if you hope to stay even, much less to get ahead. This commandment just doesn't take into consideration the hectic pace of life in the twenty-first century." You make a point that every busy person can understand. But consider this. The fourth commandment is grounded in God's rest following creation. A job that anyone would think impossible was completed in just six days, and God did it so thoroughly and perfectly that He rested on the seventh day of that creation week. Why can't you learn to work like that? What's stopping you from learning to rest like that? Why can't you learn to trust God like that with the chaotic pace and demands of your life?

Let's face it: there's grave danger in the way most people put life together today. Tom Attridge was once a test pilot for Grumman Aircraft. He also holds the distinction of being the only pilot in history who shot down his own airplane. He was flying an FII jet fighter in 1956 during its development. Flying at supersonic speed over the Nevada desert, he fired the cannon mounted under his plane's wing and then, a few seconds later, ran into the very shells he had fired. The jet was simply traveling too fast and brought itself down.

No other incidents like it have been recorded in the history of military flying. Unfortunately, however, lots of lives have crashed and burned as a result of flying too high and moving much too fast. I learned this past week that the Chinese pictograph for the concept of "busy" is composed of two characters: "heart" and "killing." That's what being overly-busy does: it kills the heart, both the muscle that beats in your chest and the spirit that animates your life. Doctors have identified a whole batch of anxieties, depressions, relational breakdowns and occupational health and safety issues caused by lack of sleep and overwork. Are you "busy" like that? How are you doing at keeping up with everything going on in your life?

This commandment is extremely relevant to our busy, fast-paced, 24/7 lives. God has established a rhythm for us: work hard, it's good for you; then rest a little, it's absolutely necessary for you!

Third, and finally, the Sabbath "is a day of rest dedicated to the Lord your God"(Exodus 20:10). That doesn't mean, as some interpreted it in the past, that you should do absolutely nothing on the Sabbath except go to church. In fact, the only thing the Bible specifically prohibits on the day for rest is work! In that sense, I suppose that the fourth commandment is a license to goof off one day a week; which, I think you'll agree, isn't a bad commandment at all. On the Sabbath, God wants you to kick back, relax, enjoy yourself, celebrate life and God's goodness. He never intended to inflict misery and boredom upon His people or to deny the pleasure of a day off from work.

However, it is important that you understand that whatever you choose to do on the Sabbath, you do not leave God out of it. In fact, the commandment requires that you put and keep God at the very heart of it! It's a day dedicated to the Lord! There are many ways to factor God completely out of the Sabbath. Listen to me, though. The Sabbath is a day to restore eternity to your soul! That's why gathering with the people of God to worship God is such a crucial part of the Sabbath. Don't you remember:

Jesus Himself never missed worship on the Sabbath(Luke 4:16). Even He needed what it offers!

Given the pace of your life and all the demands upon you, God knows that you have little time during the work week to devote to worshiping or serving Him. Therefore, if you don't do it on the Sabbath, you'll wind up leaving God completely out of your week. Then, after you've done that for a few weeks, you'll discover that you've pushed Him completely out of your life. And that's when things will begin to fall apart!

The Sabbath is a gift to us from God. It's okay to relax and take it easy one day a week. It's just not okay to push Him out of it. You can relax in His presence. He's completely safe to share your life with. More than anything else, God just wants the time to be with you, unbusy, unobligated time to enjoy you, to show you His love. He just wants a little of your time to show you how to live all the rest of your time!

That's what the Sabbath is all about!

HONOR YOUR FAMILY

"Honor your father and your mother, so that you may live long in the land the Lord your God is giving you."
(Exodus 20:12)

A man from Phoenix calls his son, Tom, in Atlanta on the day before Thanksgiving and says, "Son, I hate to ruin your day and your Thanksgiving, but I have to tell you that your mother and I are getting a divorce. Forty-five years of misery and marriage is about all either one of us can take."

"Dad, what are you talking about?" the son asks.

"I'm telling you," the father responds, "we can't stand the sight of each other any more. We're sick of one another and I'm sick of talking about it, so call your sister in Chicago and tell her."

Frantic, the son calls his sister, who explodes on the phone. "There's no way they're getting divorced," she tells her brother defiantly. "Don't worry, I'll take care of this."

She calls Phoenix immediately and before her father can say a word, she announces, "You are not getting divorced. Don't do a single thing until I get there. In fact, I'm calling Tommy back right now and we'll both be there first thing tomorrow. Don't do anything until we get there. Do you understand me?" Then she hangs up.

The father hangs up his phone and turns to his wife with a broad and satisfied smile on his face. "Okay, it worked" he says, "They're both coming for Thanksgiving and what's more, they're both paying their own way."

It's an amusing story because there's so much truth in it. Many parents are cut out of their children's lives once the children leave home and are occasionally even tempted to trick their kids just to get them to pay a visit.

This sermon continues the series through the ten commandments plus one and brings us to the fifth commandment which calls the people of God to honor our fathers and our mothers. Immersed as we are in a culture of fragmented families, it may be difficult to appreciate how seriously the Bible takes this obligation. The first hint, though, that we're given about the importance of honoring our parents comes from the position of this fifth commandment among the original ten.

The scriptures tell us that the commandments were given to Moses on two stone tablets(Exodus 32: 14). Jewish tradition says that the first tablet contained the first four commandments, the ones dealing exclusively with our relationship to God. The second tablet, headed by this one spelling out our obligation to our family, contains God's instructions for getting along with our fellow man, the primary concern of the remaining six commandments. By its very position, then, commandment number five, becomes the key to understanding the proper balance between our relationship with God and our obligations to others.

For instance, notice first the promised consequences that go along with this commandment: proper respect and honor within the family yield a positive impact upon society in general, and the people of God, in particular. That's the meaning of the words that follow the basic command, " ... so that you may live long in the land the Lord your God is giving you." It's the only commandment with an attachment like that, a point that does not go unnoticed by the Apostle Paul when he quotes the fifth commandment in the New Testament. He writes, this is "the first" - and we might add, the only - "commandment with a promise "(Ephesians 6:2). In other words, this commandment is about so much more than good manners, proper respect, and the simple politeness of children toward adults. This commandment indicates that the destiny of a nation and civilized society - and we might even add, the future of the church - hinges largely on the nature of the relationship between parents and their children.

Not long ago, a mother of two adult children who's become wiser than she thinks through experience and reflection, commented that one of the most important things that parents should teach their children is how to accept supervision, take direction, and submit to authority. You see, no matter how important or successful you may be, no matter how smart or clever you are, no matter how much you may assert your independence or your stubbornness, no matter if you believe that no one has a right to tell you what to do, and whether you like it or not, there will always be someone, some law, or some regulation over you to which you must learn to submit. Just ask Sammy Sosa, Martha Stewart, or the corporate executives of World Com, Enron, or the New York Times.

The scriptures indicate that there are three basic sources of human authority in life, in addition to the authority of God. Those three basic human authorities are: the home, the church, and the government. Here's what the Bible says about them: "Make the Master proud of you by being good citizens. Respect the authorities, whatever their level; they are God's emissaries for keeping order .... Exercise your freedom by serving God, not by breaking the rules. Treat everyone you meet with dignity. Love your spiritual family. Revere God Respect the government" (1 Peter 2: 13-17). In other words, God has established patterns of authority for the orderly functioning of human life and it both pleases and honors Him when we willingly submit ourselves to them.

And where do people learn how to do that? The family is where we begin to learn about authority. It's in the relationship between ourselves and our parents that we either learn to respect authority or to scorn it. What we learn in our family either serves to equip us to live effectively in the real world or it cripples us so that we will eventually fail in other relationships, in our civil responsibilities, and even in our careers. You see, there'll always be people who exercise authority over us, and the way we treat our parents is most likely the way we'll treat every other authority figure in our lives.

It all begins with a father and a mother. If we don't establish a healthy respect for authority and submission toward parents in the home, if we don't learn where the lines are drawn, then we're all certain to pay a pretty high price later on. Listen to me, parents. Children who talk back, show disrespect, can't do what they're told when they're told to do it, cry, scream, shout until they get their own way and rebel, aren't cute. Instead, they represent the earliest and first warnings, of devastating storms to come. On the other hand, when parents teach the lessons of authority effectively, and when children learn them well, those children will move forward toward fulfillment and success. It all begins at home, and that's the very thing that this commandment promises.

Finally, understand what the proscribed requirements of this commandment: honor those through whom God gives you life. The word "honor" literally means "a heavy weight." No doubt, you've heard people referred to as "light weights" in some particular area of life or experience. By referring to them that way, you mean that their advice and attainments don't really count for very much with you. Even though you should probably listen to them out of sheer courtesy, you shouldn't necessarily feel obligated to mold your life after the pattern they've laid down. They are, after all, "light weights." They haven't earned significant or decisive influence over you by their own example or experience.

On the other hand, you may refer to a few other people as "heavy weights," and, in doing so, you mean, of course, that they are people to whom you would gladly grant influence over you. They are of heavy weight, monumental, and significant stature in your eyes. If you could be like them, you would gladly come under their tutelage and instruction. Well, that is the honor with which children should look to their parents. Essentially, the commandment urges children of all ages not to trivialize or minimize their parents' influence or to marginalize or ostracize their parents from their lives.

The most interesting thing about this fifth commandment is that it establishes no time limit and no age limit for the honor that children owe to their parents. In other words, there's something in this commandment for everyone! Carol talks to her Dad every Sunday afternoon and I've never told her the joy that I find in their conversations. Carol still calls him "Daddy" and she always says, "Yes, sir" and "No, sir" in responding to his questions. My wife honors her Daddy. I can tell that she always has; after all these years, he still carries heavy weight and significant influence in Carol's life, even though she's grown, gone, and become very independent. She's not obligated to obey him anymore, but he certainly receives - and deserves - her honor.

We all need to learn how to honor our parents in the different stages of life. In both Ephesians 6:1 and Colossians 3:20, the Apostle Paul gives his commentary and insight into the meaning of this commandment for children. In those two scriptures, he writes, "Children, obey your parents because you belong to the Lord, for this the right thing to do, ... this is what pleases the Lord." To be obedient to your parents means that you listen to them with the intent of understanding them so that you can obey them and follow their instructions. If you're still living under the same roof as your parents, and if you're not yet independent of their support and their provision, and if you aren't obeying them, then you simply aren't keeping this commandment. For children, then, honor primarily means simple obedience.

For young adults who've become independent of their parents, honor means appreciation for the very best of what their parents taught them. As you grow older, you'll begin to see the weaknesses of your mother and father, all their hang-ups, neuroses, and idiosyncrasies that you never noticed before. It'll be easy to see all their faults and it'll even be tempting to become angry, even bitter, and to throw out everything they ever taught you. You'll be inclined to do practically everything your own way. It's good that you're becoming independent, but you don't have to do so at the expense of throwing away the best things your parents taught you and did for you.

The scriptures remind us to keep our parents' " ... words always in your heart. Tie them around your neck. Wherever you walk, their counsel can lead you"(Proverbs 6:21). The scriptures remind us to develop the character our parents prayed and longed that we would have. The

The Ten Commandments

Bible urges us to make them happy and proud that we're their child, and to never give them cause to be ashamed of us. Proverbs 23 reads like this: "Listen to your father, who gave you life, and don't despise your mother's experience when she is old. Get the truth. .. also get wisdom, discipline, and discernment. The father of godly children has cause for great joy. What a pleasure it is have wise children. So give your parents joy! May she who gave you birth be happy"(vs.22-5). For young adults, then, honor primarily means to appreciate and to be grateful for your parents.

The Bible says that to honor your father and mother is a lifelong commitment. From the day a child is born until the day his or parents die, everything in that relationship changes except the duty of honor. How do you do that continue to honor your parents after you have your own family? For one thing, it means that you start giving back. It means that you stay in touch with your parents as long as they are alive. It means that you respect and speak well of them, even when they're frail, even after they're gone. It means that you speak kindly to them and kindly about them. It also means that you meet their needs, just as our Lord did when He was dying on the cross. One of the last things He did before He drew His final breath was to make certain that His mother was cared for(John 19:26-27).

So, here's the fifth commandment: "Honor your father and your mother .... " It doesn't matter whether you're young or old. It doesn't matter if they were perfect or not. It doesn't even matter if they're still alive. "Honor your father and your mother ... " and then you can expect God to make good on His promise: if you honor them, just as the Lord tells you, you'll live a long life, one filled with His blessings! What's more, the world will become a much better place!

Amen.

RESPECT LIFE!

"You shall not murder." (Exodus 20:13)

A third-grade Sunday School teacher was teaching the meaning of the fifth commandment, "Honor your father and mother." "Does anyone know a commandment for brothers and sisters?" she asked. One little girl raised her hand: "Oh, I know! I know!" When the teacher called on her, the little girl responded with an obvious frustration in mind, "Thou shalt not kill!"

While little girls may, in fact, often be tempted to take matters into their own hands when it comes to their annoying little brothers, most of us know that the significance of this commandment stretches far beyond establishing limits for venting natural impatience with younger siblings. The truth is, this has become the most debated of all the 'Ten Commandments.

Animal rights' activists have taken the sixth commandment as a blanket prohibition for killing any living thing, including dangerous animals, poisonous snakes, or pesky insects; hunting, fishing, and the humane slaughter of animals for food; and some even argue for prohibiting animal research for the treatment and cure of deadly diseases. You may remember that one of the great missionaries to Africa was Dr. Albert Schweitzer who spent his life there spreading the gospel and building a great mission hospital in Lambarene, Africa. Dr. Schweitzer took this command so literally that he forbade the killing of even so much as a fly or mosquito. Yet, at the same time, the good doctor and his associates were there in part to save lives from illnesses carried from person to person by the very insects they were dedicated to protecting. Beyond the animal rights' groups, others have vehemently argued, on the basis of this commandment, against capital punishment and war.

Perhaps it stems from the fact that some translations, including both the King James and the Revised Standard Versions, render this commandment in its broadest sense, 'Thou shalt not kill. " In the Hebrew language, there are at least seven different words that mean "the taking of life." The particular word used in this commandment, however, is never used in connection with the killing of animals, the execution of criminals, or the killing of enemies that occurs during a just war. The fact is, the Old Testament nowhere prohibits the killing of animals, capital punishment, or war. The Hebrew word for killing in this commandment is used only in connection with the killing of one human being(s) by another; what's more, it is used in the scriptures only to describe a violent death committed by any living thing against a human being. Therefore, that which this commandment prohibits is the unjust taking of any human life, along with any violent act which may result in the taking of any human life. In the scriptures, these acts are considered murder, and even in the oldest copies of the Old Testament, it takes only two words to make clear God's will regarding those acts: "No murder!" So, in fact, the commandment does not read, "Thou shalt not kill, " but "You shall not murder!"

You'd think that would settle it, once and for all, wouldn't you? However, the violence which characterizes our culture clearly indicates that we neither understand nor are inclined to order our lives according to God's Word. The times in which we live demand that we take a closer look at this sixth commandment and renew our commitment to honor and to obey it.

First, we need to understand why murder and violence are wrong (Genesis 9:6). The Bible has a simple rationale for prohibiting murder, even though it's not stated as a part of this commandment. However, God set forth His rationale long before He gave the Ten

Commandments. It's found in the story of the Great Flood near the beginning of Genesis. The reason God decided to destroy humanity was because human beings had filled the earth with violence (Genesis 6:13). When Noah, his family, and the animals that God had saved came out of the ark following the flood, God gave them specific instructions on how to avoid a future similar calamity(Genesis 9:1-17).

He repeated all the commands that had been given to Adam and Eve: human beings were to reign over creation, subdue it, and populate the entire earth. He also gave a few new instructions. Before the flood, God allowed people to eat only vegetables. After the flood, human beings were permitted to kill and eat any creature on the earth. However, one creature was to remain protected. In Genesis 9:6, God said: "Whoever sheds the blood of man, by man shall his blood be shed; for in the image of God has God made man. " God didn't direct this command only to Noah and his family, but to all the creatures that came out of the ark(Genesis 9:5). The death penalty, then, applied to any person or animal guilty of killing a human being. The reason for this was set forth clearly: among all living creatures, human beings are special. Human beings are different from any other created thing because we bear the image of God. No person has the right to take a human life because the murderer would be destroying the only thing that bears the image of God on the earth.

The basic reason for the commandment against murder, then, is one of respect: first and foremost, respect for God, because God's nature is still reflected in every human being. Killing another person is an insult to God, just like spitting at the president's portrait would be an insult to the president. Second, murder is prohibited out of respect for human dignity. We are not just another living creature among all living things. We are something different, something much better. The image of God dwells in each of us and it is His image that makes us more valuable than anything else in all of God's universe. We are the most glorious masterpiece of our Creator's genius. Even Jesus affirmed the priceless worth of human beings when He pointed out how, out of His abundance, God provides for every living thing. Then, Jesus asked: "Are you not much more valuable than they"(Matthew 6:26)?

Alex Sanders campaigned for the office of Governor of our great state last year. In 1992, he delivered the commencement address at the University of South Carolina; his daughter, Zoe, was a member of that graduating class. In his speech, Judge Sanders recalled that Zoe had a pet turtle when she was three years old. He came home one afternoon to find her dissolved in tears: her turtle had died. As best he could, he tried to comfort her. First, he suggested that they would get another buy another one just like the one that was gone. Even though she was only three, Zoe knew that a turtle isn't a toy and there's no such thing as getting another one just like the one that died. Living things are irreplaceable.

Finally, in desperation., Sanders suggested they have a funeral for the turtle. Zoe didn't know what a funeral was, so he tried to explain. "A funeral is a great festival in honor of the turtle," he said. Zoe didn't know what a festival was! So, he tried again. "A funeral," he explained, "is like a birthday party!" Now, she understood, and he was finally getting somewhere. Zoe was even getting excited at the prospects of having ice cream and cake and lemonade and balloons, and all the children in the neighborhood over to play. Her tears dried up almost instantly. Zoe was her happy, smj1ing self again. It was a wonderful day after all!

But, then, an utterly unforeseen thing happened. They looked down, and 10 and behold, the turtle began to move. He wasn't dead after all! In a matter of seconds, he was crawling away as lively as ever. And for once, Judge Sanders was struck dumb. He didn't know what to say. But Zoe appraised the situation perfectly and instantly. With all the innocence of her tender years, and with a wonderful party very much at stake, she looked up at her father and said, "Daddy, let's kill it!"

We chuckle at Zoe, but we know that our society has come to treat human life very much like she was willing to treat that turtle's life. When someone interferes with our pleasures and plans, when someone gets in the way of something we desperately want, the most popular solution is to get rid of them any way we can. That's why violence fills our land. It explains why assisted suicides and so-called mercy killings are increasingly debated in judicial, legislative, public, and even family circles: if it's too troublesome to let someone live, then let's make it legal to end their life! It's the motivation behind most of the abortions in this country: if a life interferes with somebody's plans, then it's all right to just get rid of that life.

Listen. That God created humans as the supreme beings on earth carries enormous implications. Of all that God made, nothing in this universe is more valuable to Him than a human being. Perhaps, before another calamity of Noah's-flood proportions happens again, we need to renew our focus on the worth of a human life as well as the quality of that life. Every human being is priceless to our Creator.

Finally, we need to understand how Jesus interpreted this commandment(Matthew 5:21-26). Good people like us have an aversion to killing; but then again, most people seem to be repulsed by even the thought of it. Have you ever heard that the guns of those who died at the Civil War's Battle of Gettysburg were examined later and found to have several charges of gunpowder pressed into the barrel? Apparently, everyone lined up for the fight. Every soldier raised his weapon. But not everyone fired. In fact, a majority of guns were never fired. In obedience to the next command, though. another charge was put into the barrel and it was raised again. Yet most were never discharged then either. You see, hand-to-hand, face-to-face combat, looking into the eyes of the one you could easily kill, created an aversion to killing that filled many of those soldiers, even in that horrendous situation. You see, God wires us in such a way that makes it very difficult for one person to kill another.

Jesus knew that His followers typically were not the murdering kind. That's why, in the Sermon on the Mount, He didn't dwell on the issues we seem to dwell on today; He focused instead on the issues we'd rather ignore. He told His followers that murder is, first of all, a matter of the heart. It's a spiritual issue. And whether we've ever actually taken another life ultimately dodges the real issue. God looks upon the heart, and the sixth commandment has to do with what's in our heart, as well as what characterizes our actions.

For instance, in Matthew 5:21-26, Jesus focuses on human anger. Have you ever lashed out at someone, called them demeaning and deriding names? If looks could kill, how many people would've been strewn along the path you have travelled? Have you ever lied about someone, simply made up something, stretched the truth about, or kept quiet about someone or something, when if you had spoken up, it could've helped them? Have you ever done any of those things just to get somebody out of your way, out of your life? That's the kind of thing that Jesus is talking about in this passage.

Clarence Darrow once said, "I have never killed anybody, but I've certainly read a lot of obituaries with glee." Many of us are like that. We'd never take anybody's life, but at the same time, we'll not hesitate to help ruin them, nor are we always sad when bad things happen to them. Some awful things said by some Christians about Christians have been published in The Augusta Chronicle the past few weeks. I can't imagine that our God's heart hasn't been completely broken by the way God's people sometimes act and often talk.

My brothers and sisters in Christ, murder isn't just an action. Murder is also an attitude, and some of God's people need to get their hearts and their attitudes right!

Amen.

KEEP MARRIAGE SACRED

"You shall not commit adultery." (Exodus 20:14)

Did you ever hear of the "Wicked Bible?" Twenty years after the King James Version of the scriptures was published, Charles I of England commissioned a "new and improved" translation of the Word of God. It later became known as the "Wicked Bible" because of a single printing error in Exodus 20:14. In that edition, the seventh commandment, read: "Thou shalt commit adultery." Obviously, it was a great embarrassment to the King, who immediately ordered all copies recalled and destroyed. He also imposed upon the printers a rather stiff fine of 3000 pounds, a hefty sum in the seventeenth century.

The other commandment, that is, the original one, the "You shall-not-commit-adultery "-one, may contain only five words, but those words encompass a huge topic. In fact, those few words from the Ten Commandments form the bedrock of biblical morality and summarize the whole of the scriptures' teaching on sex and sexuality. You don't have to look far, though, to realize that for many in the twenty-first century, including many who claim to be Christians, the seventh commandment has become little more than a virtually forgotten relic of an ancient and irrelevant past.

If marriage, family, and society are to survive, however, we must renew our acquaintance with, and our commitment to honor and to keep, the seventh commandment. So, let's look more closely at what "You shall not commit adultery" meant in the Old Testament world, and then at how Jesus clarified God's original intention in giving this commandment.

First, let's look at what adultery meant in the Old Testament. You might be surprised to learn that the Old Testament world was much more permissive and liberal in its understanding of adultery than ours. In fact, you don't have to read much of the Old Testament before you discover how crude and unsophisticated was the understanding of human sexuality in that part of the world at that time.

You will remember that Abraham, Isaac, and Jacob each had concubines(Genesis 16: 1; 30:7), the equivalent of a modem-day mistress or live-in surrogate mother. In the Old Testament world, a wife's primary duty was to produce male descendants for her husband; if she failed to do that, then he was permitted to father offspring by a concubine.

Even after the commandments were established, many prominent figures in the Old Testament routinely had several wives and some had very open and public relationships with prostitutes. For instance, the scriptures indicate that King Solomon had "seven hundred wives ... and three hundred concubines"(1 Kings II:3). However, the scriptures also indicate that his wives and concubines were the beginning of his downfall because "they turned his heart after other gods"(v.4). Samson was known for his sexual escapades in the boudoirs of the Philistines(Judges 6). In the view of the Old Testament, so long as a man did not sleep with another man's wife, he had not committed adultery, no matter how widespread his philandering. You'll remember that David's most public sin, and the one which brought the longest-lasting consequences, was his adultery with Uriah's wife, Bathsheba, followed by his subsequent arrangement of Uriah's death so that he could marry her.

In that part of the world, adultery was a sin committed against a married man; it was never a sin against a woman, including a man's own wife. The law declared - note the tenth commandment(Exodus 20: 17) - that a woman was counted among a man's property and possessions, alongside his livestock and servants. So, in the

Old Testament, adultery was a violation of the property law. It's primary concern was a husband's right to have children who were unquestionably his own. His wife's adultery with another man seriously compromised the husband's right to that confidence. In fact, it was considered such a serious violation of the law that both the adulteress and the adulterer were put to death(Leviticus 20:10; Deuteronomy 22:22).

Now, by the time of Jesus' ministry, the practices of concubinage and multiple wives had been discontinued. But the double standard still existed. The woman was still regarded as the man's property. She had no rights, no legal standing of her own! Adultery was still considered an offense against a married man, but not a woman; not even against a man's wife.

In the Sermon on the Mount, Jesus objected to the uncivilized and inhuman treatment of women; not just married women, but women in general, who were treated by men as property to be owned, traded, or discarded! In Jesus' view, to treat anyone as merely a sex object is sinful even if that woman is your wife, or that man is your husband! In other words, on the basis of our Lord's understanding and teaching, it is possible for a man to be guilty of adultery even with his own wife! It's even possible to be guilty of adultery when no physical sexual act has been committed. In the eyes of our Lord, adultery is any attitude which demeans, disgraces, debases, or humiliates the worth and integrity of another human being!

So, let's look at how Jesus re-defines the popular understanding of adultery and how He elevates the relationship between men and women to a new level of sacredness(Matthew 5:27-30). In the process, He sounds an ominous warning to those who use sex to control, dominate, and manipulate another human beings. His warning is to husbands and wives who have little or no contact, virtually no meaningful relationship, with each other outside the bedroom. He calls them to recapture the holy element of intimacy and love which is at the heart of every Christian marriage.

His warning is to unmarried men and women who share a sexual relationship intended only for those who are married to each other. He calls them to a serious re-evaluation of their commitment to their Lord and to each other. He reminds them that physical intimacy alone is never an adequate foundation upon which to build an enduring relationship.

He warns teenagers and young adults for whom sex is merely a form of recreation, or a way of relieving boredom or acting out their deeper needs. He reminds them that when sex is used merely as a means of holding on to a boyfriend or a girlfriend, it becomes a destructive force of exploitation that is the root of lust and adultery.

No, Jesus does not prohibit a casual, polite, or admiring glance at a beautiful woman or handsome man. Lust is much more serious than that! Generally speaking, lust refers to any all-consuming desire. Whenever any urge becomes so powerful that it dominates every waking thought, lust has taken hold. If you have trouble concentrating on anything else other than the one thing you want most right now whether it's fame or fortune, a new car or boat, a new house or business, a promotion or recognition, a romantic relationship, or merely a friendship with another person - if you would do almost anything - to have what you want, if you are tempted to risk everything you now have in order to get what you don't have, you are at the mercy of lust!

In Matthew 5:27-30, Jesus focuses specifically on the danger of lust when it becomes attached to human sexuality. When that happens, lust distorts and perverts everything else. A lustful person lives in a perpetual sexual stew. Sexual thoughts and urges dominate the mind, determine behavior, and infiltrate practically every conversation. Lust is not normal sexual desire! It is instead, the all-consuming, selfish and insatiable preoccupation with other people primarily as sexual objects.

It's easy to recognize lust. It characterizes the men and women with whom you work or go to school, the ones who seem to have nothing else but sex on their mind. Everything they say, every joke they tell, has an erotic twist. Lust distinguishes men who fall allover themselves and embarrass their wives by their behavior in shopping malls, restaurants, and other public places as they gawk at every young, attractive, fashionably dressed female they see.

Lust can also be described as friendship between married men and women, who are not married to each other, but to someone else. They'd never intentionally be physically unfaithful to their spouse, but the basic content of their secretive conversations with each other, the essential substance of their friendship, centers around flirting, teasing, and sharing their most intimate fantasies and desires, their most personal frustrations and problems with their spouse. Lust motivates the "sneak peek" at pornographic materials at bookstores and newsstands. Lust drives much of the business in DVDs and video tape rentals and purchases. Lust entices grown men and women, and teenage boys and girls, and younger, toward Internet sites that offer the basest and most demeaning and inhuman acts of a sexual nature. And it's lust that is at the root of thoughts you would never express, thoughts you can't even believe that you think.

Lust is serious business! It's humiliating and shameful, and it really shouldn't be trivialized, snickered at, smirked over, or smiled about. The Bible doesn't dismiss it nearly so casually as the wife who gives here husband permission to look so long as he doesn't touch. The Bible doesn't excuse or dismiss it with a flippancy based upon the argument that everybody lusts, everybody occasionally looks, and even looks again.

The Bible says that lust is one of the most dangerous problems we face. James, the brother of Jesus wrote: " ... Each person is tempted when he is lured and enticed by his own lusts. The lust when it has conceived gives birth to sin; and sin when it is full-grown brings forth death, destruction, and our downfall" (1 : 14-15).

As far as Jesus is concerned, lust in any form - but especially when it is connected to our God-given sexuality - is deadly business. In fact, He told His followers to avoid it as the most extreme cost. "If your right eye causes you to sin, " He said, "pluck it out and throw it away; it is better that you lose one of your members than that your whole body be thrown into hell. And if your right hand causes you to sin, cut if off and throw it away; it is better that you lose one of your members than that your whole body go to hell"(Matthew 5:29-30).

Obviously, Jesus didn't mean for you to take that advice literally. After all, removing the offending eye or hand wouldn't necessarily remove the sinful thought from your heart. His point was to underscore the necessity of taking drastic action in dealing with the lustful look and the adulterous thought. You can't nurse and pamper it, flirt with and enjoy it, tease and trifle with it, because it will turn on you and be your ruin. The only alternative is to ruthlessly root it out of your life.

Dealing with it may cause you as much pain as physical amputation. It may mean breaking off a relationship which has become meaningful to you but which is detrimental to your marriage and family, or your spiritual well-being. It may mean getting help for your addiction to sexually-explicit, pornographic materials. It may mean that you and your spouse have to seek counsel in order to recover and restore the romance and intimacy to your marriage. It will mean that you have to exercise more self-control and discipline over your thoughts and conversations. It may even mean that you have to start running with a different crowd!

Ultimately, it means that you will have to surrender your whole life to the Lordship of Jesus Christ. It will mean that you give Him permission to renew your mind and control your thoughts. It will mean that you will allow Him to change the way you talk and the way you act, even how you think. It will mean that you permit His power to change you and to make you an-entirely new and different person! It may be the most painful thing you have ever experienced, but it's the only way you'll ever really be changed!

BE HONEST

"You shall not steal." (Exodus 20:15)

This is a true story, just as it was told to me this past week by one of our senior adults on himself. Sammy wasn't very old, but he was certainly old enough to know better. When he went to visit his Aunt Tama one day, he noticed 35 cents laying on her kitchen table: it was payment for her newspaper that week. In fact, she planned to pay the delivery boy when he brought that afternoon's paper.

After Sammy went home, the 35 cents was missing. Aunt Tama called her brother, Sammy's father, and mentioned that the money had been laying out when the boy arrived but when he left, the two coins, a quarter and a dime, were gone. So, Sammy's father asked, "Son, do you know anything about 35 cents that was laying out on your Aunt Tama's kitchen table?" "I don't know anything about it," young Sammy replied. "Empty your pockets, boy," said his dad, and when Sammy did, there was the 35 cents.

The Ten Commandments

The father took his son straight to the boy's bedroom whereupon, Sammy recalls, his dad laid a mighty powerful spanking on him. "That, son," his dad said, "was for taking the 35 cents." Then, as he resumed the corporal punishment with even harder licks, his father said, "And this is for lying to me about it!" When 1 called my friend and asked if I could tell his story, he said, "You sure can, Pastor. That whippin' taught me a lesson I've never forgotten."

You might think that most adults, particularly Christians and other church-goers, have outgrown the need for a sermon on the eighth commandment. Perhaps, in a more mature and perfect world, we would have. Perhaps, in a more mature and perfect world, this might be the shortest sermon in the series on the ten commandments, plus one. Unfortunately, the fact remains: stealing is still a problem in the twenty-first century, among boys and girls, men and women everywhere. The truth is, it is a timeless issue and that's why God gave this eighth commandment. So, let's look at it more closely and see how it applies to our lives today.

First, let's be sure that we understand what the commandment actually says. You have to admit that on the surface, it's actually pretty simple and straightforward: "No stealing." Since it's likely that no one here has ever robbed a bank, mugged a stranger, or stolen a car, this commandment must surely be about someone else, but certainly not about any of us.

But wait a minute! The eighth commandment acknowledges the importance of our stuff, our personal possessions. Even in the Bible, things are considered to be good. Things are signs and symbols of blessing. If they weren't, there wouldn't be anything wrong with ripping off our neighbor's personal property. Our belongings express who we are. They demonstrate what we value and hold important. That's why we get that queasy, sick-in-the-pit-of-our-stomach feeling when something is stolen from us. Have you ever been the victim of a robbery, a break-in, or a theft of any kind? If so, you feel violated as if someone has trampled on your soul. You're diminished by having something of personal significance taken away from you.

According to the FBI, there are more than 10 million acts of theft and robbery in the United States every year. Many are unbelievably bold and brazen. Why, when I was a teenager, someone stole my Pastor's car one night during prayer meeting. He was actually preaching when we all heard the engine start just outside the small sanctuary. Of course, none of us knew until the service ended that it was the pastor's car. How much bolder than that can you get?

Sometimes that feeling of being violated isn't due to a criminal act. Maybe when you were away at college, your mother threw out something that was of real value to you and you still haven't forgiven her. When our girls were small, Carol smocked most of the outfits they wore. One Christmas, she was passing along to one of her sisters who was raising her own little girl all of those clothes in which Carol had invested so much of herself, her love, and her time. They were in a bag by the front door but somehow, in all the chaotic aftermath and cleanup from Christmas, they were taken out with the trash and never seen again. That was fifteen or so years ago, but remembering it still generates that sick-in-the-pit-of-our-stomach feeling.

So, the eighth commandment is really about respecting other people's property, too. "No stealing, " it says. It doesn't say what you won't steal, when you won't steal it, from whom you won't steal, or why. It simply means that you won't take anything that doesn't belong to you from anyone at any time for any reason.

Beyond that, it also means that you'll respect what is someone else's, you 'll respect their right to have it, and you 'll respect and take care of it if your ever find it outside the owner's care of if the owner ever commits it to your care or your responsibility. God's Word says:

"If you see your brother's ox or sheep straying, do not ignore it but be sure to take it back to him. If the brother does not live near you or if you do not know who he is, take it home with you and keep it until he comes looking for it. Then give it back to him. Do the same if your find your brother's donkey or his cloak or anything else he loses. Do not ignore it"(Deuteronomy 22:1-4). That is what the commandment states is required from God's people.

Practically, though, and in a culture radically different from the one in which this commandment was originally given, there is much more to this commandment than meets the eye. In fact, it's amazing the number of ways that people can steal. I looked up the word "steal" in the dictionary and came up with twelve synonyms. Most people I know would never think of going into someone's home and taking their possessions. That's stealing! But there are varieties of ways in which people rip off other people. Let me give you five ways that we do this. There are lots more.

First, from God's perspective, taking things that will not likely even be missed, things large or small, is stealing. We have no right to take anything just because it is of relatively little value. Pilfering, snitching, picking up that which is simply lying around, what appears to be something to which no one has a claim, is stealing. Taking a grocer's grape, or one of his plumbs or peanuts, without paying for it, is in its strictest form, stealing. Using company postage for personal mail is stealing. Sneaking your six-year-old into an event that is free for children 5 and under without paying for them is stealing.

Here's a good rule of thumb: if there is a charge associated with something, or even a personal or sentimental value attached to something, and you take it without paying for it, or you take it without permission of its owner, whether it will ever be missed, you're stealing. On the other hand, if there is clearly no charge for it and you take it without paying for it, or if you take it with permission and the full knowledge of its owner, and it is intended to be taken, it is free. Are there biblical grounds for this rule of thumb? I think so. "Do not have two differing measures in your house - one large, one small. You must have accurate and honest weights and measures, so that you may live long in the land the Lord your God is giving you" (Deuteronomy 25: 1415).

Second, from God's perspective, taking things either tangible or intangible is stealing. A good example is cheating or stealing answers from a classmate, claiming the results of his or her hard work and study as your own. This past week I read about a college athlete who was caught cheating. He sat next to an honors student. The professor became very suspicious because their answers were always so similar. But the conclusive evidence carne when the honors student answered a question on a quiz with an honest, "I don't know." The athlete answered the same question by writing, "Me neither."

Some people who would never steal a piece of equipment, not even so much as a paper clip, from their employer, think nothing of calling in sick when they're not, taking longer lunch hours than allowed, or doing personal business on the company computer. Biblical grounds? Sure. The scriptures teach us that "no one should wrong his brother or take advantage of him. The Lord will punish men for such sins" (1 Thessalonians 4:6).

Third, from God's perspective, taking things from "good guys" or "bad guys," even from those we think can most afford it, is stealing. Robin Hood was famous for stealing from the rich and giving to the poor. That doesn't make it right. That includes the IRS or a store that charges outrageous prices or even when it's just someone we don't like. None of that makes any difference. What makes the taking of something stealing is not who owned it, but the fact that it was taken without permission and without paying for it.

There's a prevalent perception in our culture that insurance companies are fair game because they're so big. They charge such outrageous premiums - and why do you think that is so? - and they have so much money that it's okay to inflate one's claims and get some money back that way.

Consider what the scriptures say about stealing from bad guys, even from those who would seem to be able to "afford it:" "Teach slaves to be subject to their masters in everything, to try to please them, not to talk back to them, and not to steal from them, but to show that they can be fully trusted, so that in every way they will make the teaching about God our Savior attractive "(Titus 2:9-10). Not even slaves are justified in stealing from their masters. That teaching must extend to the policy holders of insurance companies, as well as the citizens of a nation who demand services and protection from the very government who collects those taxes. Didn't Jesus say, "Give to Caesar what is Caesar's, and to God what is God's"(Matthew 22:21). Didn't the Apostle Paul write: "Give everyone what you owe him: if you owe taxes, pay taxes; if revenue, then revenue; if respect, then respect; if honor, then honor"(Romans 13:7). Can there be any reasonable or legitimate question in the minds of God's people with regard to what He expects from us?

Fourth, failing to return something to its owner is stealing. One of the most subtle forms of stealing is borrowing something and never returning it. Wow! How many of us are guilty of that? Do you have something that you borrowed from someone else, something that you've had for months or even years? An extension cord? A yard tool? A kitchen utensil? A serving bowl? A book from the library? A hymnal or Bible from the church? A video, tape, or DVD? You never intended to keep it, but you just never got around to taking it back. It belongs to somebody else, but if you borrowed it and have kept it long beyond the time you used or needed it, if you've had it for months or even years without returning it, it's a form of stealing! You ought to take it back today!

Finally, the scriptures label as theft and outright robbery those decisions to deprive God of what rightfully belongs to Him. You know how hard it is to look squarely in the face that neighbor or relative from whom you borrowed something months or even years ago. You'd rather do anything than have to face them when you return what's rightfully theirs. But it's the right thing to do, and you know it!

Doesn't it strike you as a bit ironic that we can take something which belongs to God and then enter His presence without any embarrassment or shame? You see, God accuses many of His own people of robbing Him, some who would never think of-stealing from anyone else. "Will a man rob God? Yet you rob Me .... You ask, 'How do we rob You?' (And) God answers, 'In tithes and offerings. (In fact), you are under a curse - the whole nation of you - because you are robbing me"(Malachi 3:8-9). This is hard, I know, and many of you don't like to hear it. Yet every time that we fail to acknowledge that everything we have and all that we are belongs to God, we are robbing Him.

I am absolutely convinced, upon the authority of God's Word, that no job in the church would ever go begging, no financial need would ever go unmet, and the economic stress gripping our nation would be resolved if God's people weren't stealing from Him. The tithe of every one of your possessions, every stock in your portfolio, every dollar in your pocket and in your bank account, belongs to the Lord, and when you tell Him, "You can't have this," you're keeping from God what rightfully belongs to Him. What's more, you're forcibly keeping shut the floodgates of heaven which could release uncalculated blessings upon you, this nation, and God's church.

Directing his words specifically to followers of Jesus, the Apostle Paul wrote: "He who has been stealing must steal no longer, but must work, doing something useful with his own hands that he may have something to share with - that is, something to give to - those in need"(Ephesians 4:28). Do you believe that that is in the Bible?

Do you believe that the Bible is God's Word?

Do you believe that followers of Jesus are to obey God's Word? Then, let us each begin today, with new resolve to obey every command He has given us!

Amen?

TELL THE TRUTH!

"You shall not give false testimony against your neighbor." (Exodus 20:16)

In the fourth century, Augustine, the devout Christian bishop of Northern Africa, said that there were eight different kinds of lies. In the twentieth century, Mark Twain, notorious for his wild and fantastic imagination, along with a radical tendency toward exaggeration, said that there are 869 kinds of lies. Who really knows?

What we do know is that lies and deception run the gamut. Perhaps you heard about the wife who noticed that her husband had given up his regular Saturday rounds of golf. She innocently asked him one weekend, "Honey, why don't you play golf with Ted and your other friends anymore?" Her husband replied, "Would you play golf with a . man who moved the golf ball with his foot when you weren't watching?" His wife immediately responded with a note of shock, "Well, of course not. I never would." Her husband said, "Well, then, you'll understand. Neither will Ted or the other guys." You see, it's not possible to get along with each other and live in harmony if we cannot trust each other or rely upon one another's word.

It may be quite impossible to identify all the ways we practice deception or even measure the full impact of lies upon the human community. In Atlanta not long ago, a minister noticed a group of boys outside his church, surrounding what looked to be a stray dog. "What are you fellows doing?" the minister asked as he approached. "Telling lies," one of them replied. "The one who tells the biggest lie gets to take this dog home." The minister was shocked and said to the boys, "When I was your age, I would never have thought of telling a lie for anything." The boys looked at each other, each one with a look of dejection and apparent guilt on his face. Finally, one shrugged his shoulders, pointed to the minister, and said, "Well, looks like you get to keep the dog, mister."

The scriptures leave little doubt how God feels about dishonesty and deceit, duplicity and falsehoods. Among the many biblical references is Proverbs 6:16-19 which identifies seven things that are detestable to the Lord: second in the list is "a lying tongue, " and next to last is "a false witness who pours out lies." Jesus calls the devil "the father of all lies "(John 8:45). The Apostle Paul follows suit when he raises the bar of expectation for followers of

Jesus: "Each of you, " he writes, "must put off all falsehood and speak truthfully to his neighbor"(Ephesians 4:25).

Perhaps nothing, though, speaks of the importance of the truth to God like this ninth commandment Imagine! Here is one of the Ten Commandments, one of the ten most important things God wants to say to the human race, one of the ten things that God intends to be preserved through all the ages for all people, and it's about telling the truth, specifically about other people. Let's look more closely at the ninth commandment.

First, let us consider what it actually says and what it meant in its original context. The commandment reads: "You shall not give false testimony against your neighbor. " In other words, you shall not say anything about anyone else that you know, or might have reason to suspect, is not the truth, ever! Frankly, this commandment should make everyone of us gulp every time we read it. Who of us has never repeated as fact, something for which we lacked credible proof or knowledge? At one time or another, we are all guilty, sadly some more frequently than others, of violating this commandment by telling something about someone that we do not know for certain is the truth.

Actually, the ninth commandment established an important Old Testament legal principle. If a person was caught in an act that violated any part of the law, at least two witnesses were required to convict him or her. "One witness is not enough to convict a man accused of any crime ... he may have committed. A matter must be established by the testimony of two or three witnesses "(Deuteronomy 19:15).

With regard to capital offenses - that is, those violations of the law requiring the death penalty - the Old Testament legal code went even further. "On the testimony of two or three witnesses a man shall be put to death, but no one shall be put to death on the testimony of only one witness. " Then it goes on. Get this: "The hands of the witnesses must be the first in putting him to death, and then the hands of all the people "(Deuteronomy 17:6-7). Do you know why the first people to throw the stones were to be the witnesses that testified against them? If later, the person stoned was found to be innocent, then the witnesses against him were guilty not only of lying, but of murder as well.

You see, the crime of false witnessing was taken very seriously. If you lied and the accused was innocent, then you would be punished without mercy. Not only that, but you would receive the same punishment the accused received - even if it was the death penalty - if your lies were the reason for his destruction. In that way, the law served as a deterrent: people were warned to tell the truth every time they saw what happened to people who lie.

It was this principle which was at the root of Jesus' teaching about judgment in the Sermon on the Mount. He said: "Do not judge, or you too will be judged. For in the same way you judge others, you will be judged, and with the measure you use, it will be measured (back) to you" (Matthew 7: 1-2). Not only that, it was this principle which Jesus followed when He held out a stone to the accusers of the woman caught in adultery. Holding in front of each one, Jesus said, "Here, if you are a without sin, then you be the one to throw the first stone"(John 8:7). What did they do? One by one, they quietly disappeared: they realized that with the throw of the stone, they were condemning themselves. Do you see how radical is God's demand for the truth?

The ten commandments call upon individuals to live uprightly and in conformity with God's laws. However, the first concern of the ten commandments is not with any individual's well-being. Their first concern is establish and to preserve a community, a society, and a culture of like-minded people who are building up one another and who are united in their devotion to God and to fellowship. As important as personal character and integrity are in all the matters addressed by the commandments, God has in view the effect of the your and my behavior on the whole body of God's people. Specifically, with regard to the ninth commandment, He wants us to realize that deceit and lying take a toll on all of us! It hurts everybody! It always has! It still does!

That's why God detests lying and deception so much. People's lives are often ruined by things that are said about them which are not true. Many of you know from first hand experience that relationships -business, personal, family, marriage, and even church - simply cannot survive deceit. And yet, at the same time, it goes far beyond that.

For instance, do you know the name Jayson Blair? For five years, he was a reporter for The New York Times, the world's most powerful newspaper. He was fired several weeks ago for plagiarism, that is stealing other people's work and claiming it as his own, but he also admitted to just "making up" a lot of his stories and interviews. It cost him his job. "He should've been fired!" you say. Well, it also cost Howard Raines, a top-ranking editor of The Times, his job. "He should've been fired, too!" you respond. Have you thought, though, what the entire episode cost you and me? The ultimate toll of yellow journalism is skepticism and cynicism, along with doubt, suspicion, and mistrust of all that we read and listen to. Look at us: that's precisely who we Americans have become.

We don't trust politicians: they lie to us! We can't believe journalists: they make up stuff! Many even doubt what they hear from the pulpits of the land. We don't even believe each other anymore! That's the toll of dishonesty and deceit! And that's why God is so concerned that we tell the truth! When people can't believe each other, marriages, families, churches, and society fall apart!

Second, let us consider how to become more truthful and honest people. Suppose I told you that every conversation you had this past week, whether at home or at work, with a neighbor or a waitress, had been tape recorded. How would you feel if that were so and the tape could be played back for everyone to hear? What would be heard? Would there be truth? Kindness? Encouragement? Or, would there be lying, criticism, gossip, or character assassination?

Actually, scientists have long suspected that every sound ever made in the history of the world, including every important speech or conversation, or every incidental and insignificant word ever uttered, is floating around "out there" somewhere and, with the proper equipment, could be retrieved and played back for everyone to hear. Even if you doubt, that man will ever possess that technological capability, even if you pray with all your heart that God will not let it ever happen, you must still deal with what our Lord said. Jesus said that there is a record of every word that you and I have spoken, not only during this past week, but every word we have ever uttered. " .. .1 tell you, " He said, " ... men will have to give account on the day of judgment for every careless word they have spoken"(Matthew 12:36).

In a strikingly similar passage, Luke quotes Jesus: "What you have said in the dark will be heard in the daylight, and what you have whispered in the ear in the inner room will be proclaimed from the roofs"(l2:3). You may deny and try your best to distance yourself from the things you have said, but the scriptures promise that a day is coming when you and your words, true or untrue, will be reunited and all will hear! Now, that ought to make every one of us gulp really hard!

What did Jesus mean He talked about "every careless word?"
Well, let's look again at the ten commandments for a clue. In Exodus 19: 16, the Hebrew word rendered "false" actually means "groundless." Groundless words have no basis in fact, meaning, of course, that a false witness brings an accusation or charge that has no basis in reality. It makes no difference as to the intent of the false witness - he may intend to harm or destroy a person, or make himself feel or seem important, or goes along with the crowd, or simply repeats a rumor - he has no substantial grounds or basis of fact for his claim. He is being "careless"

with the truth. He is not guarding carefully enough what he says.

In Deuteronomy 5, the Old Testament's "other version" of the ten commandments, another word for "false" appears: in the original Hebrew language it actually means "frivolous: "Do not bear frivolous witness against your neighbor"(v.20). That means "careless" as well. Any reckless shooting off of our mouth in order to put down or damage the reputation of another person qualifles as bearing false witness against our neighbor and puts us in danger on judgment day. Jesus says, " ... By your words you will be acquitted, and by your words you will be condemned"(Matthew 12:37).

Listen to me, brothers and sisters. You may not pay much attention to the things you say, the way you talk, the words you choose, the rumors you repeat, or the gossip you spread. But upon the basis of God's Word, I tell you that the Lord notes every syllable that comes out of your mouth. And whatever your intent when you utter those words, ultimately it will do you more good or harm than the one toward whom it is directed.

Abraham Lincoln once asked a man he was debating, "How many legs does a cow have?" The disgusted reply came back, "Four, of course!" Lincoln agreed. "That's right Now, suppose you call the cow's tail a leg, how many legs would the cow have then?" The opponent replied smugly, "Why, five, of course!" Lincoln quickly came back. "Now, sir, that's where you're wrong. Calling a cow's tail a leg doesn't make it a leg!" My friends, lying doesn't change the truth!

The only thing your words truly reveal is what is the nature of the spirit that lives within you. Jesus said, "out of the overflow of the heart the mouth speaks"(Matthew 12:34). Amen!

LEARN TO BE CONTENT!

"You shall not covet your neighbor's house. You shall not covet your neighbor's wife, or his manservant or maidservant, his ox or donkey, or anything that belongs to your neighbor." (Exodus 20:17)

It's not the kind of thing you would expect to hear out of any small South Carolina town. On Sunday night, July 6, an 18-year-old girl allegedly ran down her ex-boyfriend and his 17-year-old date outside the Oakbrook Movies 8 theater in Summerville. Witnesses said the pair was hit by a car going at least 50 mph. The 17-year-old-girl died at the scene, her date was rushed to the intensive care unit at the Medical University of South Carolina, and the driver was taken away in handcuffs, charged with murder and assault and battery with intent to kill. She faces life in prison but is also eligible for the death penalty, if convicted.

Some will say that it was an insane jealous rage that prompted the 18-year-old to commit such a senseless act of violence. No doubt, that will be argued at her trial. However, the scriptures identify a sin with a long history of shockingly similar and equally devastating results as her motivation. In the language of the tenth commandment, the Summerville tragedy was the extreme consequence of one girl coveting what another girl had. What's more, what happened in Small Town, South Carolina, is the predictable outcome of unchecked and unbridled coveting in its most radical expression. Besides that, it poses a lurking, very real, but still largely unrecognized, danger to us all. That's why we need to examine the tenth commandment more closely.

Let's start by considering what the scriptures mean by coveting. How do you define it? Most people will use synonyms like envy, greed, or jealousy. Some might use words like materialism, lust always wanting something else, or never being satisfied with what you have. A few might even suggest that coveting means wanting something so much that you are willing to do anything to get it, even run down someone else who has exactly what you want.

The Old Testament is filled with real stories of real people who covet so much what others have that they are willing to turn their backs on God, betray their own family members, steal, lie, commit adultery, murder, and in every other way disregard, trample down, and literally run over anyone who gets in their way, simply because they are determined to make what they want their own. Coveting shows up early in the Bible. In fact, it is at the root of the first sin(Genesis 3:1-7). God places the first man and woman in a garden paradise where every need is met. Yet, He also places in the middle of that paradise a forbidden tree. The couple is free to eat anything they want in the garden; they just cannot eat from that one tree. Enticed by Satan, though, the woman reaches out for that very thing that God does not want the two of them to have. She wants it. She covets it. She believes that she needs it in order to be personally fulfilled. She tells herself that without it, there will always be an emptiness inside her. Without it, she will never be all that she can be. So, she grabs it and then gives it to her husband and that's how the sin of coveting becomes firmly established in the human heart.

Another familiar biblical story about coveting is about twin brothers, Esau and Jacob(Genesis 25:24-34). Esau is his dad's favorite son and Jacob is mama's boy. It seldom takes any more than that to act as a bait that always arouses coveting. You see, Esau will kill for the love of his mother, and Jacob will lie, steal, deceive, trick, and betray his own blood for the approval of his father. Coveting is the cruelest of all sins because it does not even respect family!

Coveting was the downfall of some of Israel's most powerful people. As King, Ahab was able to have anything money could buy. He specifically wanted to buy Naboth's vineyard and made a fair offer for it. The vineyard, though, had been in Naboth's family for generations and he was not inclined to sell. Ahab was understandably disappointed, but then he began to act very childish about the whole thing. He sulked and pouted, even refused to eat, because he was so obsessed with what he could not have. Finally, his wife, the queen, took matters into her own hands. She bribed two scoundrels to bring false charges against Naboth, charges which resulted in his death. Then the queen seized the property and presented it to her husband. Not only was he guilty of coveting, but he also became party to lying about his neighbor, stealing, and murder(1 Kings 21).

David was guilty of another kind of coveting. He didn't want someone else's property or money; he wanted another man's wife(2 Samuel 11). The king's fascination with Bathsheba led him to commit adultery with her. After that, he attempted to cover it up by killing her husband, Uriah. What had begun as coveting ended in adultery and murder. In the cases of these two powerful kings, an initial breach of the tenth commandment led progressively downward and eventually resulted in their violations of the sixth, seventh, eighth, and ninth commandments as well. That's the way coveting works: it's like a very small spark that suddenly erupts and blazes out of control, consuming and destroying everything and everyone within its reach.

So, what is coveting? As these four Old Testament examples clearly demonstrate, *coveting is wanting what was never meant or made for you.* It is desiring what someone else has, even in terms of special relationships with other people. Coveting creates un-resolvable tensions and misery within families, causing the deepest and widest rifts between parents or siblings, even driving husbands and wives to betrayal and adultery. It generates overpowering obsessions that cause a grown man or woman to act childish and irrational, and to make good judgments impossible. Coveting feeds on feelings of inadequacy, emptiness, and self-pity!

I remember a wife who once came to me with a cartoon of Dennis the Menace. As she handed it to me, she said, "That's my husband!" In the cartoon, Dennis is thumbing through a Toys 'R Us catalogue saying, "This book's got a lot of things I didn't even know I wanted!" Then she described how her husband's insatiable desires for what others had in terms of possessions, achievements, power, and the appearance of success had driven them to the brink of bankruptcy and family disaster.

The scriptures realize that coveting taints and tarnishes, ruins and destroys everything significant and meaningful in life. It is all covered by the tenth commandment. Read it again: "You shall not covet your neighbor's house. You shall not covet your neighbor's wife, or his manservant or maidservant, his ox or donkey, or anything else that belongs to your neighbor"(Exodus 20: 17). That is a pretty sizeable challenge!

In fact, let's consider how the New Testament describes the challenge presented by coveting. *First, this commandment is unique in that it deals more with what's in our heart than with what we actually do or how we act out in our conduct and behavior.* Think about it. All those words that you used to define coveting, weren't they more descriptive of attitudes, of ways you feel inside you than they describe ways you act? Envy? Greed? Jealousy? Emptiness? Wanting something really badly? Those are things about you that you hide, that you try desperately hard to keep a lid on. Those are secrets that you don't want anyone else to know, a side of you that you don't want anyone else to see!

Well, this is where the Christian faith gets really hard. You see, Jesus knows better than we do that every sin is committed twice: first in the heart and then in action. Don't you remember what He said? "What comes out of a man is what makes him 'unclean.' For from within, out of men's hearts, come evil thoughts, sexual immorality, theft, murder, adultery, greed, malice, deceit, lewdness, envy, slander, arrogance, and foolishness. All these evils come from inside ... "(Mark 7:20-23). The fact is, nothing stays in the heart. Nothing stays hidden, closeted and secret, private, personal, and unrevealed forever: whatever the hidden sin in your heart, you may be certain that it will fight and claw with all its might until it eventually gets out! That's why Jesus dealt so straightforwardly with coveting: "Watch out!" He said. "Be on your guard against coveting; a man's life does not consist in the abundance of his possessions"(Luke 12:15). In other words, you can get and gain more and more "things," you can acquire, achieve, and accomplish more and more successes, you can move from one relationship to another, and still be empty and unfulfilled. Life does not consist in the abundance of your personal conquests and accomplishments!

Jesus even said that coveting is one of the greatest hindrances to spiritual growth. In the parable of the sower and the seeds, He said that it is "the desires for other things - that is, coveting" which chokes out the Word and makes it unfruitful in our lives (Mark 4:19). Let's not kid ourselves. That's the great danger for us all, that we will become so distracted by, obsessed with, and possessed by things, that there will be no room left in our lives for God's kingdom!

The brother of Jesus, James, writes: "What causes fights and quarrels among you? Don't they come from your desires that battle within you? You want something but don't get it. You ... covet, but you cannot (ever) have what you want. (So) you quarrel and fight"(James 4: 1-2). Tell me: how many relationships have gone sour for you, not because of something someone did to hurt, harm, or even alienate you, but because of an attitude that developed in your own heart toward them? How many of those attitudes had something to do with something you wanted that they had: friends, happiness, things, health, children, a marriage or mate, recognition in the community or on the job? Don't you see, James says that coveting sets more relationships at odds than practically anything else. When an attitude turns from an "I-want-something" to an "I-want-yours," it becomes exceedingly destructive. When an attitude turns into an "If-I-can't-have-it-I-don't-want-you-to-have-it-either" obsession, everything is ruined! All that comes of that is constant quarreling and fighting!

So, what are followers of Jesus to do? If coveting is crippling you, if it's making you miserable, if it's brought you to the brink of personal ruin and destruction, is there any hope? How can you overcome it? Well, I do have some good news.

Apparently, the Apostle Paul identifies with us in this struggle. He writes: "I once thought all these things - money, power, prestige were so very important, but now I consider them worthless because of what Christ has done. Yes, everything else is worthless when compared with the priceless gain of knowing Christ Jesus my Lord I have discarded everything else, counting it all as garbage "(Philippians 3:7-8). In other words, in his own thinking and life experience, he simply switched the price tags. The things he once thought were most valuable, he came to discount; and the things that he once thought mattered hardly at all- Jesus, spiritual truth and reality - he came to see and to value as priceless! Really, that's what this commandment is all about. It just doesn't happen overnight!

Paul writes again, "I have learned to be content in whatever the circumstances (of my life). I know what it is to be in need, and I know what it is to have plenty. I have learned the secret of being content in any and every situation, whether well fed or hungry, whether in plenty or in want"(Philippians 4:11-12). How can you learn to be content with the circumstances of your life? Just like everything else that you learn, there are steps to take and habits to form. Here are two that will start you on the way to overcoming coveting and begin to move you toward contentment.

First, train yourself to be thankful for everything. Paul writes: " .. .In everything, (learn to) give thanks"(Philippians 4:6). So often, coveting unmasks the greatest dissatisfaction of all when it reveals our dissatisfaction with God's provision for our lives. You may never say it out loud, you may even deny having the thought, but a heart that covets what it does not have is a heart that is actually saying, "You've not been fair with me, God. I deserve a better job, a higher salary, a bigger house, a prettier wife, a husband more like my best friend. You've shortchanged me, God. You owe me better than this!" Don't be guilty of that: form the habit of finding in every circumstance something for which you can be thankful!

Finally, train yourself to celebrate when something good happens to someone else. We are very good in the church at helping the less fortunate and ministering to the least and the most needy among us. What we have not yet mastered is the ability to celebrate with and for others, to literally be happy and overjoyed for someone else when they receive what we would have liked for ourselves. Yet, it is an obligation given to every follower of Jesus to rejoice with others and to be thankful for their blessings! In fact, in Romans 12:15, the Apostle Paul writes that that obligation comes before the duty to be compassionate and sympathetic: "Rejoice with those who rejoice;" he writes, and "mourn with those who mourn "(v.15). It's not natural, to be sure, but with God's help and with disciplined effort, you can overcome the covetous spirit that is making your life miserable, that's dooming your relationships to failure, and that's robbing you of your spiritual joy!

Paul wrote to Timothy: " ... Godliness with contentment is great gain. For we brought nothing into this world and we can take nothing out of it. But if we have food and clothing, we will be content with that"(1 Timothy 6:6-8). The happiest people I know are those who are simply content with the things God provides. They have a genuine relationship based upon trust in their heavenly Father that brings them both pleasure and peace. They are people who are content to trust God to "provide their needs according to His riches in glory" (Philippians 4:19). In fact, they are the richest people I know!

www.ingramcontent.com/pod-product-compliance
Lightning Source LLC
Chambersburg PA
CBHW021014090426
42738CB00007B/781